THE ACA LEGAL SERIES

Volume 12

"AVOIDING COUNSELOR MALPRACTICE"

THE ACA LEGAL SERIES:

Series Editor: Theodore P. Remley, Jr., JD, PhD

THE ACA LEGAL SERIES

Volume 12

"AVOIDING COUNSELOR MALPRACTICE"

Robert L. Crawford, JD, EdD

Series Editor
Theodore P. Remley, Jr., JD, PhD

Avoiding Counselor Malpractice

10 9 8 7 6 5 4 3 2 1

American Counseling Association
5999 Stevenson Avenue
Alexandria, VA 22304

Director of Communications
Jennifer L. Sacks

Acquisitions and Development Editor
Carolyn Baker

Production/Design Manager
Michael Comlish

Copyeditor
Lucy Blanton

Library of Congress Cataloging-in-Publication Data

Crawford, Robert L. (Robert Lee), 1937-
    Avoiding Counselor Malpractice / Robert L. Crawford
       p. cm. — (ACA legal series ; v. 12)
    Includes bibliographical references.
    ISBN 1-55620-130-3
    1. Counselors—Malpractice—United States. 2. Counselors—Legal status, laws, etc.—United States. 3. Counseling—Moral and ethical aspects. I. Title. II. Series.
KF2910.P753C73   1994
346.7303'3—dc20   93-33194
[347.30633]   CIP

Contents

Biographies

Robert L. Crawford is a full-time counselor educator in the Department of Counseling, Educational Psychology, and Research at Memphis State University where he teaches courses in legal and ethical issues in counseling, career counseling, and alcohol and drug abuse counseling. He also maintains a part-time practice as an attorney in Memphis, Tennessee. His involvement in professional issues in counseling includes several years of service in consulting and conducting professional development training. He was the state counseling association licensure chair who organized and led the successful effort to gain Tennessee's first professional counselor practice credential in 1984. He received his EdD from the University of Kentucky College of Education and his JD from the Humphreys School of Law at Memphis State University. He is a National Certified Counselor, a National Certified Career Counselor, a clinical member of the American Association for Marriage and Family Therapy, a licensed professional counselor, a licensed marriage and family therapist, and a licensed attorney.

Theodore P. Remley, Jr., Series Editor, is Executive Director of the American Counseling Association. Immediately prior to assuming this position, Dr. Remley was chair of the Department of Counselor Education at Mississippi State University in Starkville. He holds a PhD from the Department of Counselor Education at the University of Florida in Gainesville and a JD in law from the Catholic University of America in Washington, DC.

Preface

This monograph is the 12th and final volume in the ACA Legal Series. The theme of this monograph is that counselors can reduce the likelihood that lawsuits will be filed against them, and increase the likelihood that they will prevail if suits are filed, by developing quality assurance plans for their counseling practices.

The past several years have seen a dramatic increase in legal claims against counselors, and the topic of malpractice has received considerable attention. Counselors' reactions to this problem have evolved over the years. At first there was considerable surprise and even anger at what was viewed as intrusions on professional practice. Next was alarm because of uncertainty concerning possible new causes of action. This uncertainty led to extreme defensiveness in some instances and passivity or even fatalism in others. However, many counselors all along have reacted, as almost all counselors now do, by adopting the stance that possible legal liability is a routine part of practicing a profession in our society, and that counselors should take reasonable precautions to avoid legal liability.

Threats of legal action based on malpractice allegations need not create a crisis for counselors. Professional counselors can create quality assurance plans for their own practices that include appropriate actions and exclude inappropriate actions, and thus make sure that the counseling services they provide are legally correct. The purpose of this monograph is to provide a guide for taking these reasonable precautions to avoid malpractice suits. This guide is not presented in any sense of practicing defensively, but rather in the sense of planning positively. The organization of this monograph provides an outline that counselors may use in developing a legal and ethical quality assurance plan for their counseling practice. Such a plan also provides routines for responding to legal or ethical complaints, thereby helping to prevent problems arising from ad hoc responses to complaints.

In developing a quality assurance plan for legally correct counseling practice, topics to discuss include awareness of issues and areas of potential liability, safeguards and procedures based on this awareness, consistent implementation of these procedures, and interpersonal skills to make these procedures viable. It is not possible to include awareness of all important issues or discussion of all pertinent procedures in any one publication, and counselors should use this monograph in conjunction with other monographs in the ACA Legal Series as well as with other related texts.

A plan to avoid malpractice must be understood as a means to an end rather than as an end unto itself. Even if stating specific legally correct behavior for every counseling situation was possible, the nature of our society's legal system is too fluid and complex to allow compliance based on a rigid set of rules. Some law professors say, only partly in jest, that they can use the same examination questions over again because the correct answers have changed since the last semester. Thus this monograph attempts to provide understanding of a system to get solutions rather than the solutions themselves, and counselors should approach it with an expectation of "learning how to fish rather than being given a fish."

The topics in this monograph are interrelated rather than discrete units. The first chapter describes the legal and ethical standards in terms of their sources, purposes, sanctions, and methods of change so that readers can understand both the nature of the standards themselves and the importance of taking appropriate action to influence establishment of desirable standards. The next chapter describes the nature and scope of malpractice. Subsequent chapters address concepts and procedures to help avoid malpractice, including understanding how to determine a reasonable standard of care, understanding how professional identity is crucial in establishing the duty of care, obtaining informed consent, and managing legal aspects of relationships with clients. Three chapters then discuss the legal and ethical issues if a malpractice suit is brought. These are followed by practice guidelines and discussion questions that can assist counselor educators, supervisors, and consultants in exploring the monograph's topics with students, supervisees, and colleagues, and in understanding the monograph's applications to counseling practice.

It has been said that some people hold their slacks up with belts, that some people hold their slacks up with suspenders, but that lawyers are people who hold their slacks up with belts and suspenders—and sometimes thumb tacks. Thus this monograph is intended as general educational information only. It is not intended as legal advice for any specific situations. It should not be regarded as legal advice or followed as legal advice.

Glossary

Amicus Curiae: Literally friend of the court. The term usually applies to persons who have no right to appear in a suit, but who are allowed to introduce arguments to protect their interests.

Case Law: The aggregate of reported court cases that forms a body of law for a particular subject. In distinguishing it from statutory enactments of legislatures, case law sometimes is also referred to as *judge-made law*. In modern times the term *case law* often is used interchangeably with the broader term *common law* because it is the courts that routinely recognize and enforce the usages and customs forming the basis for a common law.

Malpractice: Literally, evil practice, with implications of illegal or immoral conduct in professional practice. As a modern legal term, the general meaning is any unreasonable failure to carry out professional duties. Applied to specific court actions, the term means a lawsuit alleging negligence in carrying out professional duties.

Negligence Per Se: Literally, negligence as such, and descriptive of conduct that may be declared to be negligence without argument or proof because the conduct is an obvious violation of a law. Applied to counseling situations, negligence per se typically involves failure to follow a particular law that has the purpose of protecting a specific class of persons from a specific harm.

Objective Test: The process that a judge or jury uses in fact-finding to decide what a reasonable person of ordinary prudence would have done under like circumstances. The term refers to society's view of reasonableness, not any individual's subjective view.

Prima Facie Case: Literally, that the evidence is to be believed unless it is overcome by other evidence. The consequence is that an opponent must rebut the prima facie evidence in order to prevail.

Proximate Cause: Legal cause, in the sense that the actual cause was close enough for justice to allow holding the actor responsible.

Quality Assurance Plan: Planned and systematic efforts to include appropriate actions, and to exclude inappropriate actions, in order to achieve consistent, desired quality of a service.

Res Ipsa Loquitur: Literally, the thing speaks for itself. The legal meaning is that a rebuttable presumption of negligence arises upon proof that the defendant had exclusive control of the thing which caused a harm, and that the act which resulted in the harm ordinarily does not happen in the absence of negligence.

Tort: Literally, twisted or wrested aside. Legally, the term means a private or civil wrong other than a contract violation. For a tort to exist, there must be violation of a duty arising from operation of law and not merely by contractual agreement between parties.

Nature of Legal and Ethical Standards

In planning to avoid counselor malpractice, it is important to know the nature of the standards we follow. This chapter compares and contrasts legal and ethical standards in terms of their sources, purposes, sanctions, and methods of change.

Sources

The source of legal standards is society itself as manifested in national, state, and local jurisdictions. Each jurisdiction includes basic constitutional law, statutes, judicial decisions, and administrative agency regulations among its sources. Constitutional law usually does not provide a direct standard of practice for counselors, but such standards may apply to counselors who work in governmental agencies. An example is that such counselors are constrained to provide equal access to services. Statutes provide many standards for counseling practice; examples include mandatory reporting of child abuse and protection of confidentiality for certain clients. Responsibility for control over most aspects of professional practice rests with the individual states, and in past years state legislatures provided the greatest number of standards affecting professional practice. In recent years there has been a dramatic increase in the number of state judicial decisions providing a body of case law standards for counseling practice; an example is the concept of a duty to warn third parties about potentially dangerous clients. There has also been an increase in government agency regulations providing a body of administrative law setting practice standards; approval of qualified staff for state-licensed mental health centers is an example.

Professional associations historically have been the source of ethical standards. The number and sources of ethical standards have increased in recent years as associations have created specialty practice codes, and as national credentialing bodies have adopted or adapted certain professional associations' codes as their own. And, as licensure statutes have been created, state licensing boards have adopted ethical codes as part of their regulations. Counselors should be alert to the existence of whichever of these codes may apply to their practice. In some cases, credentialing boards still recognize an older version of an association's code, even though the association itself recognizes a revised version.

Purposes

Society promulgates legal standards for the purpose of promoting the public welfare and protecting individual rights. Thus legal standards deal with the minimum level of behavior that will be tolerated. As long as professional behavior does not fall below these minimums, society's purposes are met, and legal sanctions are not invoked.

Professional associations promulgate ethical standards in order to state the high aspirations of a profession. Thus ethical standards deal with the maximum level of behavior that is being aspired to. Historically, ethical standards have advanced the status of the profession by assuring the public generally and clients particularly that this profession is unique and that its members could be relied on because of their ethical imperative to serve the interests of clients. Duty to clients and duty to fellow members of the profession are intertwined. If professional behavior falls below an ethical standard, it is not merely a professional person and the client who suffer. The reputation of the profession and its members could be damaged, and other clients might suffer because of diminished trust in the profession. Consequently, professional associations jealously promote adherence to these high ethical standards, but there is no intention to equate ethical standards with legal standards.

State licensing boards' use of ethical standards can have a legal effect solely for the limited purpose of determining the status of a professional person's license issued by that board. In such cases, the ethical standards adopted by the board are not intended to have the purpose of directly or indirectly setting legal practice standards.

Sanctions

Perhaps the most obvious contrast between legal and ethical standards is in the area of sanctions that can apply to counselors who fail to meet the standards. Upon a finding of failure to meet ethical standards, professional associations and credentialing boards may issue oral or written reprimands, or may call for probation, suspension, or revocation of the membership or credential involved. Although these actions can have effects on a counselor's financial status and freedom to practice, the sanctions generally do not extend beyond diminution or removal of a status.

Upon a finding of failure to meet legal standards, however, the sanctions can extend to a counselor's property and even liberty. Courts can order a counselor to pay compensatory damages or punitive damages, or can order confinement. An example is the situation in which a court orders a counselor to divulge a client's communication when there is ethical, but no legal, protection of confidentiality. The counselor can request to be excused based on reasons such as the need for a judicially created legal protection of confidentiality for this case, damage to the counselor's livelihood, and ease of getting the information from sources other than the counselor. If the court refuses to revoke the order to testify, the counselor must comply or else face contempt of court charges resulting in possible fines or jail time.

Legal and ethical standards can coincide, exist in parallel fashion with no conflict, and exist separately with no conflict. They can also conflict. In the first three instances, counselors can and should meet both types of standards, but when legal and ethical standards conflict, counselors should adhere to the legal standards. Aside from any philosophical arguments, the greater power of the legal sanctions makes the choice clear. The professional practice quality assurance plans that counselors create should recognize the predominance of legal over ethical standards.

Methods of Change

Where the legal standard to be followed is clearly stated and recognized, counselors readily can practice in ways that do not violate that standard. However, certain aspects of our legal system create problems in determining the standard to be followed. One problematic aspect is the methods of change for standards. There are statutory standards, judicially created standards, administrative-law-based standards, and ethical standards; and according to the nature of each and their specific purposes, the methods of change are different.

Statutory standards, and the methods of changing statutory standards, are relatively easy to understand. The pertinent legislative body enacts a law after a legislator introduces a bill in keeping with the purpose of reflecting public policy or promoting public welfare. Unless stated otherwise, the law is intended to apply to the population generally rather than any specific person or locality. The bill makes its way along a rigidly defined and cumbersome path, often with considerable notice and public scrutiny. Counselors, individually or through their professional organizations, have a chance to learn about and possibly influence the legislation. When a federal law is enacted, it is published in a codebook available in any library that has a government documents section. When a state law is enacted, it is published in a codebook available in the reference departments of most public libraries of that state. Despite widespread criticism to the contrary, the language usually can be understood by the general public. The law is prospective; the dearly held societal rule of no punishment without legislation prevents retroactive application of the provisions of statutes. Typically, there is a time delay before the provisions become effective. Hence, counselors can expect to have sufficient notice in order to comply with statutory standards.

Judicially created standards, or case law, and their methods of change, are more difficult to understand. The court system does not initiate action on its own but acts only to settle justiciable disputes brought before it by individual parties. In order for a dispute to be justiciable, the individual initiating the action must show that it deals with his or her own private, substantive, legally protected interest. If the individual fails to show a private interest, he or she is said to lack standing to sue, and the court does not allow the lawsuit. A general rule is that the court system takes up disputes in keeping with its purpose to protect individuals' rights; persons concerned with public matters must seek help from the legislature.

Another feature of methods of change for case law is the doctrine of *stare decisis*, or precedent. When a court states a principle of law as applying to a specific fact situation, that principle applies to all future cases in which the facts are substantially the same, even though the parties or property involved are different. This precedent is also binding on all other courts of equal or lower rank in the jurisdiction served by the first court.

When a lawsuit is filed, it seldom comes to the attention of persons who are not parties to the suit. If counselors happen to learn about a lawsuit in which the outcome could impact their practice, they do not have a right to become involved in the proceedings. They can request permission from the court to file an amicus curiae, or friend of the court, statement. However, the court has no obligation to permit this statement or to be guided by it when it is allowed.

After a judgment is given in a case, it usually is not published in a medium easily accessible to the general public. Where it is accessible, the language and its specific meaning often cannot be understood by the general public. Perhaps the most troubling aspect of case law standards is that they can be applied retro-actively. This retroactive application is possible because of the legal theory that a judge is not really making a new law but rather finding the law that has been there all along.

Counselors might face liability because of standards that were created in cases between other parties with fact situations not drawn from counseling practice. An example is the drastic change in counselors' potential liability for clients' suicides. Only a few years ago most states followed a doctrine known as *contributory negligence*, which barred most plaintiffs from recovery if they contributed even in a minor way to their own harm. Today almost every state's highest court has overturned that rule in favor of a new precedent known as *comparative fault*, wherein a defendant can be held liable for a portion of the total damages even though the plaintiff contributed in a substantial way to his or her own injury.

Administrative-law-based standards, and the methods of change for these standards, are usually easy to understand. An enabling statute is passed, and the governmental agency responsible for its implementation is limited to substance consistent with the language of the statute and to a standard procedure allowing public input. Counselors, individually and through their professional associations, have a procedural right to make comments and a substantive right to have the agency consider the merits of their comments. An example is the regulation implementing the federal law providing confidentiality of information for clients of alcohol and drug abuse treatment centers. The regulation concerning confidentiality for minors was set as allowing one confidential visit to the treatment center with no parental notification, but requiring notification of parents or guardians upon a second visit. This rule was adopted after vigorous debate by several parties, including counselors serving this type of client. Proposed federal regulations and input procedures are printed in the *Federal Register*, which is available in libraries that have a government documents section. However, notice of administrative law processes in the states generally is limited, and counselors who wish to contribute to the creation of state regulations must be diligent, patient, and alert. Once a statute is passed, counselors who wish to participate usually need to contact the state agency to learn about the procedure.

Ethical standards, and the methods of change for those standards, are also easy to understand. The standards are developed by associations, and the methods of change are straightforward. Notice of the revision process generally is published in association newsletters, and the association bylaws generally require opportunity for both procedural and substantive participation by the membership.

In summary, this description of the methods of change for legal and ethical standards teaches us that our standards have evolved from varied sources serving varied purposes. In most instances concerning creation of legal standards, the purpose was not to give direct guidance for professional counseling practice. Consequently, it is not surprising that counselors sometimes have lamented the lack of specificity of some standards, the inappropriateness of some standards, and the probability that new standards will continue to evolve whether we like them or not.

The teaching concerning methods of change is that counselors need not be passive recipients of legal standards. Although counselors cannot control or even influence every part of the process, we can and should be active players in many ways. The first step each counselor should take is to join appropriate state and national professional associations, and the second step should be to encourage and support those associations' activism in this area. The activity suggested here simply cannot be accomplished by individual counselors; it requires the credibility and resources of an association. An example is the filing of a friend-of-the-court brief in a case that might have implications for standards of practice. The court is far more likely to allow and heed a professional association's statement than one from an individual professional person. Indeed, most counselors learn about present or prospective standards only by reading about them in professional association publications or hearing about them from association members.

Other activity should include legislative-watch activity at the state level similar to the activity now being done at the national level by the American Counseling Association. As associations become more sophisticated in this process, court-watch activity and corresponding friend-of-the-court brief filings might become feasible. Legislative activism is most important of all because statutes always take priority over standards set by courts or agencies. Rather than mere expressions of concern about standards that have evolved or might evolve, state associations should consider initiating legislative action to set appropriate standards. Such legislative action is especially important to clarify case law that sets duties but does not adequately state what behavior will discharge the duties. For example, in California, where a state court articulated a duty to warn third parties, a statute now clarifies steps that will discharge this duty. Other states also have such legislation, but not all the statutes explicitly include professional counselors among the professions covered by the statute. State counseling associations should take political action to get appropriate statutes and to assure that professional counselors are included among the protected groups.

Legal
Liability
in
Counseling

Counselors can be at risk for legal liability under several types of legal action. One is criminal court actions, which broadly relate to public wrongs; another is civil court actions, which relate to individual rights. Civil actions in tort law, and specifically negligence, are the most important legal actions to be considered. Hogan's study (1979) of 300 suits against psychotherapists found that more than 90% of the suits were brought as torts, and that more than two thirds of these tort cases alleged negligent practice. However, the cases included more than 25 types of action, including such varied causes as assault and battery, misrepresentation, libel, and malicious infliction of emotional distress. Counselors should be aware of all types because the actions are not mutually exclusive. For example, an alleged unlawful touch could form the basis for a criminal action of assault and battery as well as for a civil action breach of contract, unintentional negligence, and intentional tort.

This chapter describes and discusses contractual and fiduciary relationships, tort law in general, unintentional and intentional torts (with a particular focus on unintentional torts), crimes, and defenses.

Contractual and Fiduciary Duty

Every counselor-client relationship has elements of both contractual and fiduciary duty. A contract is an agreement between two or more parties that creates a legal relationship. The agreement can be either written or oral, and it can be either express or implied. This agreement between parties is readily discerned in practice settings where clients pay for the services. It is less discernible in not-for-profit agencies where clients do not pay for the services, but it exists nonetheless. Counselors are deemed to get some consideration, such as fees or salaries, for their services, but the consideration could be some seemingly inconsequential act such as temporary inconvenience to the client. It is easier to create a contract than popular misconceptions might lead one to believe. Contracts could be an avenue to liability as a result of charges that the counselor failed to deliver as promised. If it could be proven that a counselor guaranteed a specific outcome that did not materialize, another avenue could be a suit for breach of warranty. Another charge could be that the counselor extended or increased the amount of services in order to protect the counselor's income. In all such cases, the damages are likely to be limited to reimbursement for the client's losses. Consequently, it is not surprising that suits seeking damages based on the contractual relationship often seek additional damages based on the fiduciary relationship. Conversely, plaintiffs who commence tort actions sometimes include contract claims in order to add to the weight of their evidence and in order to increase the amount of damages claimed.

A fiduciary relationship means that it is based on trust and confidence in the counselor by the client, and it exists because the counselor has undertaken a duty to act primarily for the client's benefit by serving the client in the counselor's role as a professional counselor. Specifically, the counselor's duty is to provide care conforming to the reasonable standard of care that society expects of someone with this professional identity. Unlike a contractual duty, which can take many forms depending on the intention of the parties, the nature of a professional standard of care is not subject to negotiation by the parties. The state of mind of the parties is part of the evidence a court uses in determining what duty society expects of a member of this profession, but the subjective views of the counselor and the client are not by themselves determinative of this duty.

This duty of care cannot be contractually eliminated or reduced, even if the client wishes to do so. Because it is based on the professional status of the counselor, the duty of that counselor is not influenced by the amount of consideration received from the client. It is the same whether the client's consideration was inconvenience or whether it was a large fee payment. For any behavior related to the relationship, the duty cannot be interrupted or held in abeyance. In view of the all-or-nothing nature of this duty, it can readily be seen why dual relationships with clients are so problematic.

Tort Law Generally

A client who suffers some type of harm due to a counselor's alleged failure to provide a reasonable standard of care is likely to file a civil suit based on tort law. The term *tort* is based on a Latin term meaning twisted, or wrested away. An action in tort deals with a private wrong in which there is an allegation that one person's conduct caused a compensable injury to another person in violation of a duty imposed by law. In these suits, a judge decides whether the case is covered under an existing precedent and, if not, whether to generate a new precedent based on this case. A judge or jury then makes a decision based on the facts of the case. In understanding the application of tort law to professional practice, it is important to note that tort law continues to evolve according to its main purposes of compensation for losses, placing the burden for compensation on tortfeasors whose wrongful acts mean that they justifiably should bear the burden, and preventing future losses. The tort law approach to compensation is that costs, tangible and intangible, can be measured in money.

Regarding the decision about who should bear the burden of compensation, the classic formula is that conduct is wrongful if the burden of alternative conduct that would have prevented the harm is less than the foreseeable probability and gravity of the harm. For example, suppose that a counselor hears a client express an intention to deface the automobile of a third party. The counselor believes that the client is merely ventilating feelings and will not carry out the act, and consequently makes no warning. However, the client does deface the auto, and also injures a bystander who happens to witness the vandalism. Both the third party and the injured bystander sue the counselor for failure to issue a warning. The counselor's defense might include arguments that the burden of warning the third party was heavier than the burden of not warning because a warning might have been ignored anyway, that there was a chance that the third party might have made a preemptive strike against the client's person, that making a warning might have caused the client to carry out an otherwise empty threat, and that breaking confidentiality of this client under these circumstances reduced the likelihood that future potential clients would feel free to ventilate feelings during counseling sessions so that consequently the danger to society might be increased because the potential clients might act out their bottled-up feelings. The counselors's defense might also include arguments that the harm was not foreseeable because this client had a history of making empty threats, and this instance seemed no different from the previous times. The counselor is likely to also argue that the intended harm, defacing an auto, was not of sufficient gravity to indicate a warning. The counselor's defense might also include an argument that it was not foreseeable that a bystander would witness any vandalism, or that the client would engage in an act of violence against any person. In sum, the defendant counselor would argue that he or she should not be held liable because of the meanings that the facts give to the tort formula. The plaintiff third party and bystander are likely to make counter arguments, and the decision of the court will depend on the evidence presented.

It is the application of this formula that usually figures most prominently in arguments made on behalf of both parties in actual cases. Consequently, it should figure prominently in the quality assurance plans of counselors who are trying to avoid ever being a defendant in an actual case, and who wish to make it likely that they will prevail if they should be sued. The term *fault* often is applied to this justification. However, such fault does not mean deliberate causation, but rather that an ordinary person in these circumstances could have foreseen or should have foreseen that their conduct created an unreasonable risk to the other person.

Regarding prevention of future tortius conduct, tort law makes provision for payment of punitive damages in cases involving either intentional or reckless misconduct. It is arguable that tort law can be an even more potent deterrent than criminal law because punitive damages have the potential to be much greater than fines. A common practice has been to limit punitive damages to three times the amount of the compensatory damages. However, there is no legal reason why the amount of punitive damages cannot be many times the amount of the compensatory damages, and there appears to be a trend toward increasing punitive damages both in terms of absolute dollars and in terms of ratio to compensatory damages. Quality assurance plans to avoid malpractice can greatly reduce the likelihood that counselors might face punitive damages due to reckless behavior.

Unintentional Torts

The four elements of an unintentional tort for negligent behavior are that a duty existed, that the tortfeasor's behavior breached this duty, that the plaintiff suffered an actual injury, and that the injury was both actually and proximately caused by the defendant's breach. For a plaintiff to sustain an action, all elements must be alleged. All elements must be proved in order for the plaintiff to prevail. Almost anyone in the society can be a defendant in a suit for negligence. For example, every automobile driver has a duty to operate the vehicle in a reasonably safe manner. A malpractice suit is an unintentional tort alleging negligence in performing a duty based on a special relationship between a professional person and a client.

Existence of a duty. The first element required, the existence of a legal duty, is determined by the facts of a situation. There are two aspects of establishing a legal duty. One is the existence of a special relationship, and the other is the nature of the special relationship.

The existence of a special relationship usually is straightforward and undisputed by both parties. There was a meeting of the minds in which both parties intended the relationship to exist, and the behavior took place with awareness that it was part of the relationship. However, a problematic aspect of this element for counselors is the possibility that a relationship could be deemed to exist even though the counselor did not intend such, did not behave consistent with such, and did not expect the client to rely on the counselor's behavior as done in fulfillment of duty based on a counselor-client relationship. Counselors should be aware that it could be relatively easy for a special relationship to be created. What a counselor viewed as a casual conversation in passing between acquaintances might have been viewed by the other party as professional advice. If a suit is filed, the court will consider the facts to determine the existence of a special relationship.

Lay persons often decry the reluctance of professional persons to give free advice. Financial concerns may be part of this reluctance; we have only our time and knowledge to sell. However, prudent counselors recognize that their professional status creates the occupational hazard of a possibility of lawsuits and the occupational cost of no longer being able to engage in casual conversations with the freedom they had as lay persons. The better course of action for counselors is to avoid gratuitously giving advice that might be construed as counseling. When they do give advice of a general nature, such as in providing a public service by making an educative presentation, they should include disclaimers that the service is not presented as counseling and should not be relied on as such by any individual present.

Counselors also should be aware of a rule of law concerning rescues, which has the potential to create a special relationship. Unless a special relationship already exists, there is no duty to go to the aid of another person who is in peril. The classic example is that even an expert swimmer who has had lifeguard training has no duty to attempt to rescue a drowning person in a pool unless a special relationship exists because the expert swimmer is a lifeguard on duty at that pool. However, if the expert swimmer with no duty once undertakes to attempt a rescue, a duty is created to complete the attempt with all the skill and effort that could reasonably be used by an expert swimmer with lifeguard training. Counselors who create a special relationship by commencing a rescue attempt are subject to charges of malpractice if the attempt is either negligently performed or abandoned prior to its reasonable conclusion. Many states have enacted Good Samaritan statutes to disallow creation of liability for physicians who make rescue attempts, but it is unlikely that any of these statutes as presently written protect counselors from such liability.

Once a relationship is established, the nature of the duty is determined by the identity of the professional person. In determining this duty, a court considers the level of skill and diligence in application of that skill ordinarily exercised by persons with this professional identity. Consequently, counselors should not hold themselves out nor allow themselves to be held out to the public as having a specific identity unless the counselor is prepared to be measured by the standards for that identity.

In determining identity, the courts must first consider whether this profession is one that is recognized by society. In the not-too-distant past it could have been argued that professional counseling was not a recognizable profession for which practice standards could be stated. However, credentialing and accreditation gains during recent years make it likely that courts in any jurisdiction will recognize professional counseling as a profession that is separate and distinct from other professions such as psychiatry or psychology. The gains at the national level also make it likely that the duty will be stated in terms of national rather than local practice standards. The locality rule, in which courts determined reasonable standards in light of evidence only from the local community, generally has been abandoned. Courts today are likely to allow nationally based evidence (such as out-of-state professionals testifying as expert witnesses), nationally used texts, and scope-of-practice statements from other jurisdictions and national organizations.

Breach of duty. The second element that must be proved in a malpractice case is breach of duty, an allegation usually most vigorously contested by the defendant professional person. It also is usually the most difficult allegation for the plaintiff client to prove. The burden of proof is on the plaintiff who must prove that the counselor's behavior failed to conform to a reasonable standard. However, once the plaintiff client presents a prima facie case that is sufficient to prevail unless contradicted or overcome by contrary evidence, the defendant counselor must rebut the evidence or present a defense. Rebuttal can take the form of denying the accuracy of certain facts alleged by the plaintiff, or of asserting that the facts do not indicate failure to provide reasonable care. Because the burden of proof in tort cases is mere preponderance of the evidence, which can be satisfied by a weight even a fraction over 50%, the defendants usually present their strongest possible case. Although it is not necessary in order to prevail, the defendant's presentation usually includes evidence that the facts indicate reasonable care.

In most cases, the counselor will prevail unless the plaintiff proves negligence by a preponderance of the evidence. However, a legal principle known as *res ipsa loquitur*, the thing speaks for itself, can apply to require counselors to prove that they were not negligent when the plaintiff has already proved that the thing causing the injury was in the defendant's exclusive control, and that the injury ordinarily does not happen in the absence of negligence. An example might be an assessment report that was in the exclusive control of the counselor but that somehow has been published. If the counselor denies any negligence or deliberately taking action to publish the report, the burden is on the counselor to show evidence of reasonable care in preserving the confidence of the record. If the counselor did choose to release the record, it is necessary for the counselor to show a justifying defense such as qualified privilege in order to prevail.

In some circumstances, a rule of law known as *negligence per se* can result in a counselor's conduct being declared negligent without proof concerning due care because the conduct is an obvious violation of a law. Applied to counseling situations, negligence per se involves failure to follow a particular law that has the purpose of protecting a specific class of persons from a specific harm. An example is failure to report suspected child abuse or neglect.

An actual injury. The third element that must be proved is that the plaintiff client suffered an actual injury. If a case goes to trial, the counselor is likely to have little direct participation concerning rebutting the existence of injury. Most of this rebuttal will be done by the counselor's attorney and other expert witnesses. Counselors should be aware that plaintiffs' attorneys have become increasingly sophisticated in handling mental health cases, and they can be very resourceful in identifying injury and presenting supporting evidence. It is relatively difficult to prove the existence of injuries that are primarily mental or emotional in nature, such as loss of self-esteem and depression. Consequently, the existence of other symptoms, such as inability to sleep or jaw and teeth damage due to grinding the teeth, might be alleged both as evidence of the underlying emotional distress and as evidence of additional injury. Changes in life circumstances, such as loss of a job or spouse, also might be alleged as evidence of the underlying emotional distress and of additional injury. Injuries might be alleged as resulting from continuance or worsening of the problems that first caused the client to seek counseling. Allegations of iatrogenic injuries, which are injuries caused by the counseling process itself, and allegation of new injuries might be made as evidence of the injuries themselves and as evidence of causation.

Causation. The fourth element that must be proved is causation. There are two aspects of this element to be considered. One is cause in fact. The other is legal cause, commonly referred to by the term *proximate cause*. It is not possible to have legal cause without having factual cause, but it is possible to have actual cause but no legal cause.

Cause in fact must be established by evidence that the counselor's act or omission was a necessary antecedent to the injury. It is established only by application of the "but for" rule, which states that a defendant's act is not a cause of the injury unless the injury would not have occurred but for the defendant's act. Most occurrences in life could have many factual causes, and this statement is particularly applicable to causation of the types of injuries most often alleged in counseling malpractice suits. However, a defendant's contribution to the cause need not be the sole cause, or even the last cause, for an injury or liability to exist. The test for liability is whether a defendant's act was a material element and a substantial factor in causing the injury. If such materiality is proved, the defendant can be held liable even though there are other causes of the injury. (The extent of a defendant's liability in such multiple-cause cases depends on the jurisdiction's applicable rule of law. In some the rule is apportionment of liability according to portion of causation; in others defendants can be held liable for the entire damages even though they contributed only a portion of the cause.) Factual causation could be deemed to exist for acts of omission as well as acts of commission. Omissions can be problematic for counselors because their special expertise might be deemed to require them to recognize potential danger to a client and take affirmative steps to prevent the danger.

After the existence of cause in fact has been established, the existence of legal, or proximate, cause can be considered. The term *proximate cause* is descriptive only in the sense that there must be a legal proximity in terms of justice: it is close enough to hold the defendant liable. It is impossible to state a formula for determining the existence of proximate cause. It is always to be determined by the court on the facts of a case in consideration of any precedent applicable to the facts or in consideration of common sense, fairness, and public policy. Major factors identified as related to legal cause include, but are not limited to, foreseeability of injury, which might increase chances of finding legal cause, and presence of intervening events, which might decrease chances of finding legal cause.

Intentional Torts

The concept of intent has figured prominently in the evolution of our system of laws. Early English law did not even distinguish between a tort and a crime. Such concepts were unknown, and a harm was to be redressed or retaliated against regardless of the intent of the person causing the harm. Today the concept of intent is an important element in providing definitions for unintentional torts, intentional torts, and crimes.

Upon first consideration, counselors might not see a need to include attention to unintentional torts in their quality assurance plan to avoid legal liability because of two primary reasons. One is that they generally do not intend harm to anyone. The other is that most attention to this subject treats intentional torts as if they were limited to certain specific behaviors, such as battery, and counselors are not going to do those specific behaviors. Counselors should be aware, however, that there are four reasons why their plans should include an awareness of intentional torts.

1. The law's definition of intent is objective even though the actor's state of mind is subjective. A court can deem an act to be intentional if the result is substantially certain to occur, even though the actor did not subjectively intend the result.
2. There is the possibility of tort liability other than the common specific categories. The rule of law generally is that a prima facie case is established when the plaintiff shows that the defendant intentionally invaded a protected interest, even though protection of the interest has not already been identified as a category of intentional tort. The burden then shifts to the defendant who must rebut the evidence or else show some justification to excuse the act.
3. Actual damages do not have to be proved in order for a plaintiff to prevail; nominal damages can be awarded. This point has important implications for counselors. Intentional torts are a very minor part of the work of courts because most intentional torts are committed by judgment-proof persons (those who would suffer little embarrassment or have no money). Consequently, most potential plaintiffs in society have little motivation to sue for intentional torts. However, the possibility of vindication alone might be sufficient motivation for some counseling clients to pursue this action.
4. The possibility of punitive damages might increase the likelihood that plaintiffs will bring this action.

It is worthwhile here to discuss some of the specific categories of intentional torts. These include defamation, invasion of privacy, battery, assault, and intentional infliction of emotional distress. Counselors can use this knowledge to avoid these categories and hopefully to make generalizations that will help them avoid becoming a defendant in some case that might establish a new category.

Defamation is the offense of injury to a person's character or reputation by either oral or written false and malicious statements.

The theoretical elements are publication (communication by whatever means to some third party), falsehood, and malice. In a legal sense, malice is defined as intentionally doing a wrongful act without justification. Malice need not be proven directly; it can be inferred from the circumstances. Truth is an absolute defense in most jurisdictions, but the burden of proof is on the defendant to prove truth rather than the reverse. A small minority of jurisdictions now will find that defamation has been committed if proper motives and justifiable ends are not proved even though truth is proved.

Invasion of privacy is a defendant's offense against a plaintiff's peace of mind related to the right to be left alone. The intrusion on a protected privacy right is the only element required for the tort to be complete; there need not be any publication to a third party or any falsehood. The primary concern for counselors is that giving unreasonable publicity to private facts is sufficient to constitute this tort. Most counselors already have attended to this problem by not mailing descriptive letterhead envelopes to clients. However, counselors should review their procedures to make certain that other behaviors, such as responding to phone calls about appointment changes or allowing improper personnel to answer the telephone, do not constitute this offense.

A *battery* is a defendant's intentional and unpermitted physical contact with a plaintiff's person. The contact can have been made by the defendant's person or by something set in motion by the defendant, even though the defendant might not be aware that a contact was actually made. It can have been done to the plaintiff's body or to anything in contact with the plaintiff's body, such as an object held in the hand, such that a reasonable person will deem it an offense against the person. Although the contact must have been intended, it need not have been intended to be harmful. It is no defense that the contact was intended as a joke, as a compliment, or even to render routine assistance. The effect of this tort is to protect against unpermitted physical contact that harms even the plaintiff's dignity. For example, a counselor who hugs a client might be doing so for a therapeutic reason, such as indicating support or encouragement, but the hug nonetheless constitutes a battery if the client has not given permission for the contact.

An *assault* is an act that arouses a reasonable apprehension of an immediate battery. It is no defense that the defendant really never intended to make contact as long as there was an intent to create the apprehension. The effect of this tort is to protect against mental or emotional harm. The elements are apprehension, not necessarily fear, of the defendant's present ability, opportunity, and intent to commit the threatened battery. An offensive gesture or even an innocuous gesture accompanied by offensive words can be sufficient. However, any words that reasonably indicate merely a jest or absence of present intention negate the tort. The example of a hug can apply to this tort also. A counselor who begins, but doesn't complete, an effort to hug a client could be liable for the tort of assault.

Intentional infliction of emotional distress is a relatively new tort that has had more publicity in the popular press than court successes. Courts have been reluctant to give independent legal protection of plaintiffs' freedom from emotional distress. In order for the tort to exist, the defendant's conduct toward the plaintiff must be characterized as shocking or beyond all bounds of decency according to community standards. Generally, the subjective extreme emotional distress of a particular plaintiff is not sufficient; the circumstances must be so outrageous that an ordinary person would reasonably experience extreme emotional distress. However, counselors should know that where they are aware of special vulnerability of a client, it is possible that their conduct could be judged based on what effect it reasonably could be expected to have on that particular client.

Crimes

Counselors are at little risk of being charged with crimes based on their counseling practices, and if charges should be made, the "beyond a reasonable doubt" burden of proof borne by the prosecution makes it likely the counselor will be found innocent. Avoiding criminal charges is not likely to be extensively dealt with in most counselors' quality assurance plans, but there are reasons why some attention should be given to this topic. It has already been mentioned that the same fact situations could give rise to both tort suits and criminal prosecution. Usually, success or failure in one of these court actions has no effect on the results in other court actions. Additionally, the extensive fiscal and emotional costs of being a defendant in a criminal action make it important to become aware of possible criminal charges and take reasonable steps to avoid them. A few of these charges—

assault and battery, accessory before and after the fact, misprision of a felony, conspiracy, contributing to the delinquency of a minor, failure to report child abuse or neglect, and offering testimony in violation of a privileged communication statute—are discussed here.

The terms *assault* and *battery* already have been discussed as being separate intentional torts. Although both civil and criminal actions can be brought for the same conduct, and although there are several overlaps concerning the elements of the torts and the crimes, there are considerable differences between criminal and civil laws concerning assault or battery. There is also considerable variation in states' laws defining and naming these crimes. Criminal laws in many states have combined the two into one crime known as assault and battery or just assault. Criminal laws in most states provide for more serious charges of aggravated assault and battery in certain circumstances, such as use of a dangerous weapon. Aggravated assault also can be charged when circumstances indicate outrage or atrocity, such as attempting to have improper sexual connection, or when the victim is highly vulnerable due to age or other conditions.

Counselors often are concerned about the extent to which learning about crimes of clients or other persons can result in criminal charges against the counselors. Such knowledge might create some discomfort for counselors, but it is highly unlikely to lead to criminal charges against them. There are ways in which involvement in the acts of other persons can lead to criminal charges, but merely learning about and failing to report a client's past criminal activity generally is not one of them.

Accessory before the fact is the crime of inciting, encouraging, counseling, or commanding another to commit a crime. In most states, conviction of accessory before the fact carries the same penalty possible for the other person who actually carried out the crime, even if the other person happened not to be convicted. In this regard, counselors are reminded that there is no legal or ethical protection of communication about a crime being planned, and that failure to report knowledge of a specific crime being planned by a client could lead to a criminal charge against the counselor. For example, if a client uses a counseling session to plan a crime, and the counselor's technique includes helping the client rehearse the steps in the crime, it is possible that the counselor could be deemed to be an accessory before the fact.

Accessory after the fact is the crime of having knowledge that a felony has been committed and assisting the offender with the intent to aid the offender to avoid arrest or conviction. Giving false statements to police in order to thwart their search for the offender or making false statements at trial are sufficient for this crime. However, mere silence, refusal to cooperate with the police, or even denial of knowledge about the offender's crime, generally are not sufficient. For example, if a police investigator asks a counselor for confidential information, and the counselor refuses to discuss the client with the investigator, the counselor's action does not constitute accessory after the fact.

There is theoretical risk but little or no actual risk of criminal charges based on an archaic crime known as *misprision of a felony*, which is simply the failure to report a crime that one learns was committed. Mention of this crime continues to exist in textbooks and in the laws of a few jurisdictions, but it is highly unlikely that the charges will be brought anywhere, and even more unlikely that they could be sustained if they were brought.

Generally, counselors' conventional judgment as good citizens make it likely that they will take steps necessary to avoid being at risk of being charged as an accessory. However, certain popular misconceptions about the crime of *conspiracy* indicate that conventional judgment as good citizens might not always be reliable to make it likely that counselors will take steps necessary to avoid being charged as a co-conspirator. There are several features of the crime of conspiracy that are not consistent with other crimes and with many persons' ideas about necessary elements of any crime. Conspiracy is a crime in which two or more persons agree either to do an unlawful act or to do a lawful act in an unlawful manner. The unlawful act that is the object of the conspiracy does not have to be a criminal wrong; it can also be a civil wrong. The agreement is the essence of this crime, but even a tacit agreement can be sufficient. Mere knowledge, acquiescence, or even approval of another person's plan is insufficient. For other crimes generally, mere planning to do a crime is not itself sufficient to constitute the crime; in order for a crime to be complete there must be some action to carry it out. For conspiracy, the agreement itself can be deemed sufficient to constitute both the intent and the act.

There also are some peculiarities in procedural rules when conspiracy is charged, and perhaps the most problematic is the co-conspirator exception to the hearsay rule. Usually, the hearsay rule prohibits use of any unsworn out-of-court statement in order to prove the truth of the matter contained in the statement. However, such unsworn statements made by one person charged as co-conspirator are admissible as evidence against every person charged as co-conspirator. For example, suppose that in a counseling session a client complains to a counselor about difficulty in eating healthfully because of campus food service recipes, and the counselor states, "Yes, we ought to just stage a protest about that." The client later tells a classmate that the client and the counselor are planning to conduct a sit-in at the university cafeteria in order to protest the use of saturated fats in food preparation. If a sit-in is unlawful in this jurisdiction, and if conspiracy charges are brought, the classmate's testimony could be admitted in a conspiracy trial as evidence of the truth that both the client and the counselor made an agreement to use unlawful means to seek a lawful end.

As a practical matter, conspiracy charges are seldom brought against ordinary citizens in their efforts to achieve lawful ends. However, the possibility exists, and our society's history shows that this charge has been made against ordinary citizens who agreed to use unlawful means in seeking lawful and even praiseworthy ends. Every counseling environment has clients who might talk to a counselor about plans for taking action to stand up for their rights or beliefs, and sometimes the counselors might feel responsibility to encourage client autonomy in asserting themselves. In serving these clients, however, counselors should take care that their own statements do not lead to even an inference of agreement to seek a lawful end in an unlawful manner. The volatility of many issues, such as abortion, could lead to confrontations and subsequent criminal law involvement for ordinary citizens in a way that has not been present in our society for a generation.

The crime of *contributing to the delinquency of a minor*, broadly defined as conduct that encourages a minor to violate the law, is worthy of attention here because this volatility seems especially pronounced when minors are involved. Consequently, there might be more possibility than ever before in our society that well-meaning behavior of ordinary citizens could be deemed by other persons as conduct aimed at subverting the morals of juveniles. Laws pertaining to rights of minors and rights of parents or guardians are not settled in many jurisdictions (Salo & Shumate, 1993), and counselors should be cautious. When there is uncertainty as to what is lawful and what is not, there is less risk or error for conduct consistent with recognition of parental rights.

Two other crimes are worth mentioning because of their own importance and also because they represent the continuing evolution of both the law and the counseling profession. The first, *failure to report reasonably suspected child abuse or neglect*, has received wide attention. Most states now have laws making it a crime to fail to make such reports.

The second, *offering testimony in violation of a privileged communication statute*, generally has not come to the attention of counselors. Most states' attorney-client privileged communications statutes include creation of this crime. Some existing or proposed state counselor licensure laws incorporate by reference the attorney-client privileged communication statute for the pertinent state, thereby creating the possibility of a criminal charge for counselors who violate the statute. It is important for professional counselors to seek legislative provision for enhanced professional status. It is necessary for professional counselors to be aware of the enhanced responsibilities and liabilities that accompany such status.

Defenses

Generally, the most important defense to any charge is to rebut the evidence that alleges existence of the requisite elements. There are certain other defenses, for example, that plaintiff clients' actions indicate that they assumed the risk for their own injury, or that they contributed sufficiently to their own injury for the defendant counselor to be excused from liability under the law of the jurisdiction. However, these defenses will be raised as appropriate by the defendant counselor's attorney and do not usually lend themselves to manipulation by the counselor in prospectively establishing defenses. Two defenses that can be manipulated by the counselor, and that should figure prominently in quality assurance plans, are informed consent and qualified privilege.

Informed consent is a certain defense to any intentional torts or crimes that have lack of permission from the client as a requisite element. If the client has effectively given consent, there can be no assault, battery, or invasion of privacy. Informed consent is not a certain defense to unintentional torts. However, it is such an important factor both as a possible defense and as an element of reasonable standard of care that it is the subject of another in this monograph.

Qualified privilege, also known as conditional privilege, is a rule of law that provides a possible defense to some charges involving improper communications. It is most often used to negate the unintentional tort of violating a client's confidentiality and to negate the intentional tort of defamation. The elements of qualified privilege are good faith, a duty that can only be discharged by making the communication, and communicating only to a party whose duty or interest justifies receipt of the information. The element of good faith requires absence of malice and absence of recklessness regarding the subject matter, but it does not require that extraordinary efforts be made to verify the accuracy of information that reasonably indicates the existence of a duty. For example, if a client informs a counselor that a helpless person is being abused by a caretaker, the counselor has no duty to investigate before making a report to the appropriate investigative agency. The element of duty need not be a legal duty; it can also be a social obligation. Indeed, if a specified legal duty existed, there would be no need to apply this rule. The element of communication to a necessary party has two aspects. One is the circumstances of the receiving party that create a duty to receive the information, and the other is that the method of communication is the most reasonable one for discharging the duty with the least chance of the communication being received by other parties.

An example is the reporting of child abuse or neglect. In states that have laws establishing this specific legal duty, there is no need to apply this rule. During the period before this category of duty was created, however, the rule of qualified privilege applied to create a social obligation for a counselor or other person to report child abuse, and correspondingly protected the reporter from liability based on making the report. Further, the wording of most states' statutes includes a codification of the elements of qualified privilege. A duty to report reasonably suspected child abuse is stated. Specification is made of the party to whom the report must be made in order to discharge the duty, usually the local sheriff or a state department of protective services. The person specified to receive the report has a duty to investigate. There is a provision that the person making the report is protected from liability as long as the report is made in good faith and as long as the communication is made only to the specified party in a manner reasonably chosen to prevent disclosure to other parties. This example illustrates the underlying principle that for qualified privilege to apply, the circumstances must be such that failure to make the communication will be a greater wrong than making the communication.

Reasonable Standard of Care

This chapter discusses how to determine a legal standard of care for professional counseling practice. This legal standard is referred to as a *reasonable standard of care*, although the terms *due care* or *ordinary care* also are used.

Reasonable standard of care is a legal term broadly defined as the behavior of a reasonable person of ordinary prudence under like circumstances. This reasonable person is not an average person who really exists, but rather a composite view of society's judgment of how a person in particular circumstances ought to behave. As such, the reasonable person's behavior is not necessarily that of the majority of respectable persons. A commonly used example is jaywalking. The majority of respectable persons in a community probably jaywalk at times, but a jury might well find that an instance of jaywalking violated society's standards of safety for a reasonable person. This idealized image of a person does not require perfect behavior or perfect results; requiring such is not reasonable in anybody's view. Errors that occur are not unreasonable unless they are inconsistent with reasonable care. Errors that are inconsequential are not considered unreasonable, and are also not actionable based on a related principle of law that states that the law does not take notice of very small matters. Imperfect or undesirable results do not indicate lack of due care unless they are shown to flow from

conduct viewed as unreasonable. Consideration of the param-
eters of a reasonable standard of care indicates that it is, indeed,
reasonable.

Where special abilities are claimed by a person, such as a
professional counselor, and reasonably relied on by another
person, the standard of care is determined according to reasonable conduct in light of those special abilities. For counselors,
the standard is reasonable conduct expected of a counselor in
like circumstances. Usually, if a professional person is practicing properly in light of standards set by the profession, the
practice also meets legal standards of care. However, the standard still is set in terms of society's view rather than any
subgroup of society such as members of a profession. Consequently, it sometimes happens that all evidence indicates that
the conduct is proper according to the profession's standards,
and yet the court finds the defendant liable because the conduct
failed to meet the legal standard.

The test in applying the standard of reasonable care is the so-
called objective test, in which a jury or judge decides what a
reasonable counselor ought to have done. The term *objective test*
is descriptive in the sense that it is society's view of reasonableness that controls, not the subjective view of any individual.

Reasonable standard of care is a constant rule. However,
several circumstances make it impossible to predict precisely
what finding a jury will make in applying the standard to a
particular set of facts in a particular place and time. The facts
vary, if only slightly, from one case to another. Even if the facts
were the same in two cases, two juries in the same jurisdiction
might come to different conclusions as to what a reasonable
person should have done in light of the facts. The content and
manner of presentation of evidence might differ between cases.
Legal procedure about what evidence will get considered can
vary between cases within a jurisdiction according to a procedure known as *rule of the case* and also according to the
considerable discretion that judges have in allowing expert
testimony. The rules of law setting standards vary between
jurisdictions. Finally, existing rules within any jurisdiction are
subject to change at any time. These circumstances make it
impossible for counselors to behave in a manner that will ensure
they are acting legally.

The distinction between the concepts of discretionary duty and ministerial duty provides an additional explanation as to why counselors and other professional persons cannot limit their behavior in efforts to control court outcomes. A discretionary duty is one met only with exercise of judgment in prudent discernment of the propriety of the act to be done. A ministerial duty is one met with no exercise of judgment upon the propriety of the act to be done. The difference in these types of duty provides the major distinction between the complex responsibilities of professional persons, whose discretionary duty requires them to decide what action to take, and the much simpler responsibilities of clerical and craft workers, whose ministerial duty requires them to follow instructions. A common example is that an architect has a discretionary duty to use professional judgment in drawing plans that describe where to place a load-bearing column in a building, and a carpenter erecting the building has a ministerial duty to follow these plans.

Professional counselors are not clerical or craft workers who follow a blueprint or other set of instructions, and who can be certain their behavior is correct if they merely follow the instructions. For example, a professional counselor must use discretion in selecting a standardized instrument to assist a client in gaining insight in some area of life. The counselor could then assign a clerical worker the ministerial duty of administering the instrument exactly according to the instructions. The counselor's choice of the instrument, supervision of the clerical worker, interpretation of the results, and individual counseling sessions to help the client process the information all must conform to what a reasonable counselor would do under these particular circumstances.

Professional counselors have a discretionary duty to exercise judgment in providing due care for their clients. This task is not unmanageable when it is approached systematically and analytically.

A necessary antecedent to developing this system for some counselors is to consider whether they might have at present unsystematic or nonanalytical habits of decision making that will have to be abandoned. Some counselors use a system that omits important steps or neglects important information, and that relies on leaps of intuition to arrive at a decision. Some counselors even rely on gut feelings about a proper course of action. It is possible that these counselors often reach appropriate decisions using these unsystematic methods. However, if a lawsuit alleges that a decision indicated failure to provide due care, leaps of intuition or gut feelings are not sufficient to provide a defense. In order to prevail in the suit, the counselor is likely to have to create a systematic approach retrospectively in order to explain the propriety of the action taken. Failing to systematically consider all the factors prior to making a decision is not congruent with prudent practice. Further, it could be argued that it is less than due care to make decisions based on other than careful consideration of the factors. Counselors should use a systematic approach for some of the same reasons counselors should use inferential statistics in research and *DSM-IV* categories in diagnosis: they keep gut feelings honest, substitute tuition (learning) for intuition (without learning), provide structure for necessary steps, and require consideration of pertinent information.

Also as a necessary antecedent to implementation of a system, some counselors might need to take stock of their present knowledge in the sense of professional orientation. Counselors generally have a keen dedication to meeting the ethical responsibility of serving the best interests of clients. Toward this end, counselors generally are well prepared in terms of professional practice knowledge, skills, and attitudes to render services to clients. However, some counselors have not properly attended to development of professional orientation knowledge and skills such as scope-of-practice guidelines, counselor credentials, and relationships with other human services professions. Some few have never even developed habits of systematically considering legal and ethical implications for each area of their practice. The result is that they have strong intentions to practice in a legally and ethically correct manner, but they have weak skills to carry out the intention. The inclusion of professional orientation skills in counselor education program accreditation standards should help correct any problems in this area for the future. However, present counselors will do well to review their own knowledge in terms of the most recent CACREP standards (Council for the Accreditation of Counseling and Related Educational Programs, 1994) core area requirements concerning professional orientation, and seek professional development if any is needed.

An additional act of preparedness necessary for any professional person seeking to maintain proper practice is to maintain a mindset of alertness rather than of complacency. It is possible that even the most capable professional person could develop some tunnel vision based on past experiences that might limit awareness of emerging issues and standards.

The following 10-step system can be used in determining legally correct counseling practice. The steps themselves (as well as the ultimate decision) must be made in light of what a reasonable counselor ought to do in the circumstances.

1. **Determine whether or not there is a counselor-client relationship.** The first step in a system for meeting a legal standard of care is to consider whether or not a counselor-client relationship exists. This step determines whether or not the counselor has a duty of care.

2. **Determine the nature of any such relationship.** If a relationship exists, a close second step is to determine the nature of the professional relationship, and the counselor's professional identity is the most crucial element here. The nature of the duty, such as generalist or specialist, is determined by this step.

3. **Get the facts.** In the third step the counselor must use judgment to decide whether to proceed based on the information at hand, or whether to wait and seek further information.

4. **Consider what problem(s) need to be solved.** The fourth step is to consider what problem must be solved or what decisions seem necessary to make at this time. Identification of a problem or decision usually provides a starting point to identify pertinent issues.

5. **Identify the issues involved.** The fifth step is to identify and isolate the issues involved in the decisions to be made. Never assume that there is only one issue, or that the obvious issues are the only ones. Often a term that seems to be one issue subsumes several; confidentiality is an example. In addition, one issue often suggests others; for example, dangerousness to self suggests dangerousness to

circumstances. This step may initially seem tiresome or even confusing to some counselors, but persistent efforts make the task much easier. After all, counselors are expert in dealing with whatever issues exist. Usually, there are several issues involved in any decision. For example, consider a case involving a client who expresses ideation of harming a third party. Some of the possible issues include confidentiality of a client's communications, responsibility to promote the autonomy of the client, safety of a third party, safety of the client if a third party is warned, defamation of the client, invasion of privacy of both the client and a third party, possible reduction of any danger by allowing the client to ventilate feelings, possible increase in the danger as a result of a warning, possible increase in danger by reducing the inclination of the client to seek future counseling, and possible increase in danger to society generally if other present and future clients avoid counseling sessions due to lessened confidentiality.

6. **Seek and follow any legal standards that are squarely on point.** The sixth step is to consider whether any legal standards exist that relate closely to the issues and decision to be made. If there are, follow them. An example is child abuse reporting. There is a clear duty to report, and using discretion to choose alternative conduct based on consideration of other issues and their consequences is not allowed.

7. **For cases in which there is no clear legal guidance, consider several sources and types of standards, including hierarchy of standards, standards set by the profession, legal advice, and consultation.** The seventh step is to consider the several standards applicable to the issues if no legal standard appears to require a certain response. The issues themselves often provide descriptors for the search to locate standards, but counselors should be alert to possible applicable standards that might not be located using only the obvious descriptors. Possible sources and types of standards include the following:

   • **Hierarchy of legal standards.** The source of the standard, the specificity of the standard, and the wording of the standard all can give guidance as to whether a particular standard is intended to predominate over other standards, or whether it is merely one of many to be considered on balance. Generally, the hierarchy of written sources is statutes, regulations written in implementation of specific statutes, court cases, regulations written in implementation of general welfare statutes, statements of national credentialing boards, statements of professional associations, texts or treatises, articles in primary journals, and articles in secondary journals.

When specific cases are concerned, this hierarchy is not hard and fast but subject to many factors, including the method of getting evidence admitted into court and the credibility of the witnesses whose testimony is used to give opinions about the value of the sources. For example, a state's licensure statute is likely to control concerning a scope-of-practice issue both because of its importance in the hierarchy and because of its specificity on the point; and the licensure board's regulations on scope of practice are the next important source after the statute itself. Of course, court cases always have potential to interpret a statute in terms of such factors as the statute's legislative history or in terms of other counterbalancing issues.

- **Standards set by the profession.** Evidence of standards set by the profession are the most important source in terms of number and specificity of practice standards. It is possible to be practicing consistent with the standards of a profession and still be held liable for violating the reasonable standard of care. However, the standards of the profession continue to be extremely important in terms of evidence for a jury to use in determining reasonable practice, and the standards consequently have corresponding importance for counselors to use in judging the propriety of their conduct. In determining the overall standards of a profession, the intertwining relationship of legal and ethical standards makes it difficult to apply either type of standard in isolation. There is often room for reasonable minds within a profession to differ as to proper courses of action to take in specific situations, and each opinion is likely to be couched in terms of both ethical correctness and practice efficacy. The ethical standards of professional organizations always should be considered in seeking guidance about reasonable practice. Because the ethical standards are by their nature intended to be high aspirational standards rather than minimum legal standards, failure to meet these high aspirations does not indicate failure to meet the lower legal standards. However, meeting the high ethical standards could provide evidence that the practice exceeds minimum legal standards. Meeting ethical standards is strong evidence of absence of negligence and almost surely will rebut any allegation of recklessness. The determination of the extent to which ethical standards have been met is not always clear because written ethical standards are not intended to encompass every situation possible for counseling practice. Counselors who have questions concerning ethically correct practice for specific situations often can get guidance in the form of advisory opinions from associations' committees on ethical practice, and it is likely that these opinion statements will be given great credence by a court.

- **Legal advice.** Getting guidance concerning legally correct practice for specific situations can be a difficult and sometimes frustrating experience for counselors. At times it is appropriate or even necessary to seek legal advice concerning practice situations, but often it is not feasible to do so. One reason is the cost involved, especially if frequent advice is sought. Another is the possibility that such advice will not provide one clear direction to take. If there is only one clear direction to take, the chances are that the counselor has located it at step six. If there is a controlling standard the counselor overlooked, an attorney is likely to know it and be able to give a clear direction to take based on it. However, in the absence of such a clear direction, the attorney's advice is likely to be couched in terms of probability, and the probability itself is likely to be based on the accuracy of the counselor's opinion of the reasonableness of alternative actions to take. Yet another reason is that the advice is only the lawyer's opinion, and a court may take a different view entirely. Even a state or national attorney general's opinion does not bind a court to follow it. Courts themselves do not give advisory opinions, but render decisions only when they are deciding an actual case. One possible course of action is to seek advice from the counselor's liability insurance company hotline if this service exists.

- **Consultation.** The seventh step often requires seeking consultation from other counselors who have experience in practice dealing with the pertinent issues and similar situations. The importance of seeking consultation cannot be overemphasized. A counselor's systematic approach to legally correct decision making is not an end in itself but a means to an end, and getting appropriate consultation is an essential part of the system. In the event a counselor is accused of making an error in judgment, producing colleagues who have agreed that the actions taken were appropriate helps establish that the counselor acted as a reasonable counselor should have. The consultants sometimes have knowledge about legal and ethical standards applied to practice situations that the counselor might have missed. Their judgment about the applicability of the standards and the propriety of alternative actions always is important to consider. In addition to the helpful advice counselors can get from consultants, the process itself might be sufficient to add objectivity and prevent any reckless behavior by the counselor, and it should be proper evidence that the counselor sought to behave cautiously if a suit alleges recklessness. An inexperienced counselor should consider getting supervision instead of or in addition to consultation.

8. **Consider alternative courses of action and their possible consequences.** Typically, by the eighth step, the alternatives have been suggested by the standards and hence are already identified, but counselors should be alert to any others not yet recognized. The consideration of alternatives includes what is known and also what reasonably should be known. Likewise, the consideration of consequences of courses of action includes what is known and what reasonably should be known. The attempt to consider what should reasonably be known about either alternatives

or consequences sometimes provides new insight or information, and it always provides evidence to help rebut a
plaintiff's after-the-fact allegation that a reasonable counselor should have foreseen such.

9. **Reconsider what problem(s) need to be solved.** The
ninth step is to reconsider what problems need to be solved
and what decisions need to be made now that all the
information has been gathered. Usually, the problems and
decisions are the same ones recognized at the beginning, but
prudence dictates that they be reconsidered before making
a decision.

10. **Select and implement the best course of action.** The
tenth step is to select and implement the best course of
action from among the alternatives in terms of the balance
required by the tort formula. It is appropriate here to
reiterate the tort formula that conduct is wrongful if the
burden of alternative conduct that could have prevented the
harm is less than the foreseeable probability and gravity of
the harm. The standards identified in the seventh step
provide vital information that gives meaning to the elements of the formula. However, the decision to be made is
not merely which of the standards to follow. The decision to
be made is which course of action a reasonable counselor
should take in light of all the information applicable to the
formula.

Often the decision will not be an ideal one that solves all
the problems. Indeed, solutions to some problems create or
exacerbate other problems. It is worth noting that examples
of this clash of solutions are common enough that they often
are used in oral examinations for counselors.

Once the action is taken, it should be monitored in terms
of its effect and possible need for modification. In some
instances the action, once taken, is not readily remediable.
For example, a communication to a third party can not be
taken back once it is made. At other times the action begun
is readily remedial, as in the revision of a treatment plan.
Usually this oversight finds that the action was proper. In
any case, this continued attention often is consistent with
due care and can also allow reduction of any damages that
might occur even when errors are made.

Counselors should preserve the account of the process leading to the decision. If a suit alleges failure to provide reasonable care, the defendant-counselor's attorney needs this account in order to prepare the defense. Sometimes this account is helpful in providing information that can result in getting dismissal or a judgment on the pleadings without having to go to trial. If the case does go to trial, the plaintiff's attorney often succeeds in establishing a prima facie case. At that point, the professional counselor's attorney might choose to put the counselor's steps in arriving at the decision into evidence, probably by putting the counselor on the witness stand, as part of the evidence to rebut the plaintiff's prima facie case.

The preceding chapter on legal liability in counseling noted that counselors' quality assurance efforts to avoid malpractice should keep them from casually giving professional-seeming advice that might be deemed to create a relationship with a duty. This chapter on reasonable standard of care concludes by making a similar recommendation. Once a counselor-client relationship is established, the counselor should relate to the clients only according to behavior necessary and consistent with due care as a professional counselor. Any other behavior, however innocuous, well-intended, or unselfish it may seem to the counselor, could be construed by other persons as evidence of malpracticed counseling. One example of behavior to avoid is when a client pleads with the counselor to make a recommendation or take other action in a hurried fashion. A counselor whose good will toward the client causes him or her to make a hasty decision might later be accused of failing to exercise prudence. Counselors should remember that a client's lack of planning does not create an emergency for the counselor. Another example of behavior to avoid is when a client asks the counselor to provide transportation or otherwise act as a friend to the client. A counselor whose good will toward people generally, and toward the client particularly, causes him or her to do a good deed for a client might later be accused of exploiting the client for personal satisfaction. Counselors should remember that good deeds can be punished and relate to clients only according to a reasonable standard of professional care.

Professional Identity and Interpersonal Skills

The nature of counselors' legal duty is determined in large measure by their professional identity. The general rule regarding reasonable standard of care is that it will be judged in terms of ordinary practitioners in the field, but before applying this rule, a court must determine the nature of the field itself. The objective test of society's view of reasonableness applies to determine the nature of the relationship in the same fashion that will subsequently be used to determine due care based on that relationship; the subjective view of the parties is not determinative. Further, the reality of a person's identity in terms of training and skills is not determinative, but rather professional identity is set by how that person holds him- or herself out and consequent reasonable reliance on that identity by another person. The most commonly used example is that a person who holds out to practice as a doctor, and thereby induces another person to rely on their identity as a physician, can be held to the standard of care for practice as a physician.

Establishing the nature of a profession itself is crucial to determination of the professional duty to be discharged. A profession is defined as a vocation including attributes of practice, modified by experience, in using skills developed based on a body of knowledge, to the vital practical affairs of humankind, with an ethical imperative of service to clients (Cogan, 1955). Professional counseling leaders have been active in creating structure in professional association, ethical code, accreditation, and credentialing that give substance to claims of professional status (Remley, 1991a). The nature and stature of the American Counseling Association and its affiliated divisions, the nature and stature of the Council for Accreditation of Counseling and Related Educational Programs, and the nature and stature of the National Board for Certified Counselors all provide support for arguing that professional counseling is now a well-established profession. Ultimate legal recognition of this professional status will be made within the courts and legislatures of the various states. The passage of licensure or other practice credentials by a state is likely to have established a professional counseling identity in that state.

Counselors will do well to review the problems (Sweeney, 1991) that led to the efforts to establish professional counseling as a unique field unto itself. During the time before a clear identity for professional counseling was established, there was always a danger, made real by several cases, that a counselor's practice might be judged by the standards of some other field such as psychiatry or psychology. Counselors' present practice should reflect awareness of the teaching from these past difficulties. Professional counselors who exercise discretion in holding themselves out to the public should be able to avoid any serious difficulty concerning professional identity. However, failure to exercise discretion could result in continuing problems as courts set legal standards that a counselor subjectively did not intend.

The single most important point in establishing professional identity is usually the title used by the counselor. The title is likely to be given great weight by the courts in deciding clients' reasonable expectations and corresponding application of a particular association's ethical code and practice standards. Counselors who practice in states that define titles in terms of practice credentials, such as licensed professional counselor, should use those titles. In states that have not set titles according to practice credentials, the term *professional counselor* seems most likely to create a reasonable expectation of practice according to the standards of the American Counseling Association and its affiliates.

Counselors should avoid use of ambiguous terms such as *psychotherapist*, which do not have commonly understood and agreed on meanings. Some counselors choose to use this title or some other ambiguous title because they believe it might aid their efforts to market their services. Most counselors believe that they have a right to use this title because it describes a service they offer. Having a right to use the title could be important if a counselor is charged with violating another profession's licensure law, but using a title that asserts this right misses the point of a quality assurance plan, which is to avoid problems. If a negligence lawsuit should be filed, the plaintiff's attorney might succeed in getting expert witnesses from other professions to testify that psychotherapy is proper only within the scope of practice of their profession, such as clinical psychology, and that the plaintiff correspondingly was reasonable in relying on the psychotherapist's identity and standard of care as a psychologist. Defending against this charge is not an efficacious way to begin a lawsuit, and the problems caused by confusion of terms could be especially problematic if the case is heard by a jury having to make a decision largely based on which expert to believe. If it appears to a jury that the counselor has misled the client about the counselor's identity and corresponding skills, the counselor's attorney has a serious damage control problem in establishing that a reasonable standard of care was met for whatever profession's standards the jury believes should be used.

A related problem in terms of identity is present when counselors use titles expressing identity with one approach to counseling. The once-common practice of setting standards in terms of specific schools of thought has greatly diminished usage by modern courts, and the trend is in the direction of even less usage. Previously, a recognized school of thought, with definite principles of its own that were adhered to by a respectable minority of the profession, could form the basis for a court to determine reasonableness. Examples include psychoanalysis, client-centered therapy, and behaviorism. Counselors who choose to practice only according to a school should be aware that a court might deem their practice standards to be set in terms of a profession as a whole. Further, the determination of which profession's standards to use could be problematic.

Perhaps the second most important point in establishing the counselor's professional identity is the services counselors hold themselves out to offer. In states that have credentialing statutes and corresponding scope-of-practice definitions, counselors should adhere to those definitions in advertising their services to clients. Counselors should take care that they do not explicitly or implicitly imply abilities they do not have. In states that do not have scope-of-practice definitions, counselors should know and follow the guidelines related to national credentials. Thus counselors' quality assurance plans should include a defensible scope-of-practice statement; such should not be left to ad hoc or after-the-fact definition.

Counselors who hold themselves out as specialists have their standard of care set in terms of the ordinary skills expected of a general practitioner in the field plus the extraordinary skills and diligence expected of a specialist. One of the most common problems concerning identity is implying having a specialization when the counselor really meant to state intention to delimit practice based on limited abilities. For example, a novice counselor who is interested in careers might wish to practice only in the area of career counseling, but does not intend to hold out to practice as a career counseling specialist. When delimitation is intended rather than specialization, the prudent course of action is not to advertise or otherwise hold out to practice in terms of the limitation. Some professions use terms about practice limited to a specific area in order to indicate practice as a specialist, and this custom could be used as evidence to support allegations that a plaintiff relied on a standard of care as a specialist. Counselors who intend merely to limit practice should get explicit informed consent from clients on this point.

Proceeding cautiously and limiting practice based on limited abilities is congruent with reasonable care, but counselors should be aware that it is not possible to limit liability based on lack of skills due to inexperience. There is no distinction made on the basis of novice status in professional practice. The duty of care is set by standards for the whole profession, and novice counselors have the same duty of care as experienced counselors.

Another problem concerning identity can arise when counselors have more than one role, such as professional counselor and also as minister. Counselors should take extra care to assure that there is clear separation of these roles in holding out to offer counseling services and in performance of duties. Even when the counselor takes only one role, and consequently does not intend to have a dual relationship with a client, the counselor should make certain that there is no reasonable reliance by the client on a role the counselor does not intend. Absent explicit informed consent, for example, a client might mistakenly assume that the counselor is responding in terms of both roles at once, or in terms of either role alternatively.

It is important for counselors to attain appropriate practice credentials in order to assert professional identity. The single most important credential to determine practice standards usually is one established by the state where the counselor practices. Decisions as to what professions to recognize and what standards to set for them are left to the states, and states individually are free to establish or eliminate professions as they choose. National Certified Counselor status and specialty certifications also are important in establishing a counselor's identity. When these state or national credentials are used to form the basis of the counselor's holding out to the public, it is highly likely that their ethical codes and practice standards will be used to judge any allegation of lack of due care. Counselors also should be aware of other credentials, such as those for pastoral counselors, which the general public might think are related to their identity. Counselors must use discretion in deciding whether to seek attainment of any of the several other possible credentials. They always should use care that they do not imply unknowingly that their practice is in any way based on the other credentials.

The nature of the agency in which the practice is located can have important implications for a counselor's identity. The ownership and control, primary purpose, and funding sources of the agency, and the relationship of these to the counseling practice, all could be deemed to indicate some narrow focus, specialization, or other role of the counselor. Is the counseling practice the main purpose, or is it merely supportive or the agency's main purpose? Is it possible that the main purpose of the agency is such that the counseling service could be viewed as a means toward other ends? Counselors employed in such agencies, and who wish to have their practice identity set in terms of professional counseling, should take care to assure that this information is clearly communicated to clients, and that informed consent standards are met concerning their identity.

On a related point, professional counselors should remember that their legal and ethical duties flow from their counselor identity. These duties include being responsible to the employing agency, and the ethical codes related to specific environments recognize this. However, pressure from the agency does not excuse counselors from their responsibility to the clients. In environments where possible conflict might arise, such as a noncounseling supervisor asking a counselor to divulge a confidence of a client, counselors should have agreements made beforehand in order to avoid pressure to engage in illegal or unethical practice. When demands from an employer and standards of due care for counseling practice are not sufficiently congruent, counselors' ethical codes and legal practice standards require them to consider withdrawing from the employment.

Most of the points in counselors' quality assurance plans can operate to make it less likely that complaints will be lodged and highly likely that counselors will prevail if a legal or ethical complaint is lodged against them. However, good human relations skills also are important in avoiding malpractice suits or ethical complaints. Lawsuits and ethical complaints often are filed initially out of a sense of annoyance with someone rather than merely out of a sense of having been wronged. Reducing the likelihood of annoyances generally can have the effect of reducing the incidence of legal and ethical complaints. Counselors' quality assurance plans should always include attention to the human relations activities that counselors know so well.

Communication with the clients is important, and many of the other points addressed in a plan provide a checklist for some of the information to communicate. Early agreement on counseling conditions, agreement on client expectations, agreement on business arrangements, and keeping the client informed of present or portending changes in the relationship, especially termination, are powerful factors in avoiding complaints. Transition points are particularly important. The metaphor of an airplane ride provides an illustration. Most passengers notice and remember getting on the plane, taking off, landing, and getting off the plane more than they notice and remember the flight itself. They only notice and remember the flight if it is a bumpy one, and then they are likely to remember being reassured by the pilot's explanations on the intercom.

Counselors also should use their special communications and human relations skills to assure that only the appropriate messages are communicated. One consideration is the medium counselors might use to send a message. Discretion as to which messages are appropriately given over the telephone or through the mail should involve human relations as well as the obvious legal and ethical considerations.

It likewise is important to assure that only the intended messages are received by the clients. Some counselors' manner could possibly send an inappropriate message to clients, thereby creating unreasonable expectations. For example, a counselor's effort to provide a client with comfort and hope might be misconstrued by the client to implicitly promise better results than those explicitly discussed. Too much good cheer and optimism could also be misconstrued as implying a promise of good results. Counselors implicitly as well as explicitly should communicate that they offer a worthwhile service that has reasonable limits to what it can accomplish.

Too much friendliness could even allow clients to believe that they are to be treated as customers who are always right rather than as clients who might be confronted with information they do not want to hear. Generally, a tone consistent with a professional relationship helps prevent early unreasonable assumptions that lead to later dissatisfactions. The counselor has an ethical imperative to serve the best interests of the client, but the client is not a customer to be pleased. The counselor is a friendly professional person but not a friend. The counselor is a kind person, but the service is not being rendered as an act of kindness. Overall, the counselor respects the service being offered, and expects to be paid for it.

# Informed Consent

Counselors generally have an understanding of the concept of informed consent as well as a recognition that there is an ethical imperative to respect and encourage client autonomy. However, it is possible that some counselors are not aware of the strength and specificity of legal standards regarding informed consent.

A few counselors might even be practicing with the mistaken belief that they have considerable discretion based on a therapeutic privilege exception to the requirement of informed consent. The concept of therapeutic privilege traditionally has been that a professional person could withhold information from the client if the information reasonably could harm the client directly or indirectly by causing the client to forego needed treatment. There are some historical reasons why lore about therapeutic privilege persists. Indeed, the necessity of getting informed consent from clients prior to giving treatment is a modern concept. Many counselor-client standards have evolved from physician-patient standards, and the tradition of expecting patients unquestioningly to do what the doctor ordered, because only the doctor is capable of understanding what is good for the patient, has endured from the time of Hippocrates into modern times. Further, the duty to get informed consent largely has been imposed on medical professions by case law rather than by affirmative inclusion in ethical standards.

This body of case law standards applies to counseling practice also, and the result is that therapeutic privilege has very limited applicability to most counseling practices. Bednar and associates (1991) reviewed the case law and concluded that use of therapeutic privilege now is limited to those circumstances in which direct harm would come to the client simply from hearing the communication. Counselors should be aware that possible indirect harm to the client from avoiding treatment or having the treatment be of less therapeutic value if the client understood its nature beforehand no longer provides a basis for the use of therapeutic privilege. The trend plainly is in the direction of reduced allowance for therapeutic privilege exceptions to informed consent. When therapeutic privilege is used, the burden is on the counselor to show that its use is consistent with what a reasonable counselor would do.

A client's right to accept or refuse treatment and correspondingly to give or withhold informed consent is favored in the law. Only extreme emergencies involving possible serious physical injury create a societal interest that outweighs this right of an individual client, and this exception extends only to the time and circumstances of such emergencies. Counselors should be aware that failure to obtain informed consent itself possibly could be malpractice as a failure to recognize the right of the client to participate as an autonomous individual in decisions about his or her own treatment.

The elements of legally adequate informed consent are *competence, voluntariness,* and *knowledge.* Competence is a legal term that has several meanings; for example, there is one definition of competency for making a will, another for standing trial. Where informed consent is concerned, competence generally means the capacity of the individual to comprehend and rationally understand the nature of the procedure, its possible risks, its possible benefits, and other relevant information. Counselors usually can do nothing to create this competence; it either exists or it does not. However, counselors' quality assurance plans should include reasonable efforts to verify that the client is competent and to preserve the information that led them to conclude that competency existed. When client competency is in doubt due to minority status or incapacity, counselors should not proceed with treatment unless a properly appointed guardian gives informed consent. When it is possible to do so, counselors should get both the guardian's informed consent and the incompetent client's consent; doing so could be part of due care indicating respect for the client and promoting participation by the client.

Voluntariness also happens or it does not. Generally, absence of undue influence or coercion is equated with voluntariness. Counselors' quality assurance plans should include reasonable efforts to verify that conditions were free of undue influence or coercion and to preserve evidence of the verification. Counselors generally should not attempt persuasion or other activity to induce clients to enter into and comply with treatment. Doing so might be deemed as undue influence or even coercion. It is not possible to describe all conditions that could indicate presence or absence of undue influence or coercion. One problem, for example, might be whether clients who are coerced by third parties, such as spouses, employers, or courts, can reasonably be deemed to enter the counseling relationship voluntarily. In most such cases, it is likely that the client's choice of counseling will be deemed voluntary because the client is also free to refuse the counseling and accept consequences that might flow from the third parties. The objective rule of what reasonable persons in the circumstances would think and do applies, and counselors should exercise proper discretion.

The counselor can and should take appropriate action to satisfy the knowledge element of informed consent. Generally, clients must receive and comprehend enough information to be able to know what it is that they are consenting to. Both the nature of the information communicated and the manner of communicating are important factors in assuring comprehension, and counselors should make reasonable efforts to provide sufficient information in a manner that is comprehensible to the client. There is no one correct way to provide information, and there is no one complete list of information that always should be provided. The client's condition indicates the language, organization, speed, context, and form of the communication; the treatment indicates the content of the communication. When procedures include extreme or intrusive activities such as touching or restraining clients, or where circumstances indicate a departure from what a reasonable client might otherwise expect, such as a narrowly limited practice approach, then specific details should be provided, and they usually should be presented in writing. The following sample form includes the types of minimum information usually thought necessary to provide:

> I, Client A, affirm that prior to becoming a client of Counselor X, Counselor X gave me sufficient information to understand the nature of the counseling. This information was presented in nontechnical terms that allowed me to understand it. The information included the nature of the agency, Counselor X's professional identity, possible risks of counseling, possible benefits of counseling, nature of confidentiality including legal and ethical limits, alternative treatments available, and alternatives to treatment. I declare that I am competent to make a decision to receive counseling from Counselor X. Further, I am making this decision voluntarily; I have not been subjected to influence or coercion. My signature affirms my informed, voluntary consent to receive counseling. I am aware that I can revoke this consent and discontinue treatment at any time.
> (Statement to be added in client's own handwriting: "This statement is fully accurate. I read it carefully before signing.")
> Signature of Client A and date

This form also provides a sample of a written statement documenting informed consent. There are several points to consider about documenting informed consent. The most important one is that in almost every instance the document is merely a symbol of the process that resulted in informed consent; it is not the informed consent itself. Although it is theoretically possible to put every element of information in writing, as a practical matter some information and corresponding consent are given orally in most cases. Every counselor has a legal duty to get informed consent, and prudent counselors preserve evidence of the process. However, the evidence could take many forms, ranging from counselors' memory, counselors' notes, and short documents signed by the clients to long documents signed by the clients and witnesses to the process. There are advantages and disadvantages to each form, and there is no general agreement on what substance and form is most credible if a lawsuit should be filed. Any form could be subject to some avenue of attack by the plaintiff's attorney, and possibly could be misconstrued so as to weaken the counselor's case. Short forms, such as the one given here, might invite the criticism that they indicate the informed consent was perfunctory and thus not adequate. Long forms, which set out to state most of the information, might invite the criticism that their detailed nature indicates that the form itself was the entire process, and that certain necessary information or steps were omitted completely. Likewise, failure to have a form could be subject to attack and could be misconstrued. Counselors should consider the possible efficacy of witnesses to the documentation or to the process itself. Having witnesses could be an advantage—or a disadvantage—depending on how their use is construed or misconstrued. For example, their presence for the entire process could be alleged as evidence of undue influence or even coercion, and their absence from part or all of the process could be alleged as evidence of lack of any other part to be witnessed.

For many counselors, it is important to have a written document that can provide evidence that there was a process and that the client participated in the process; this evidence might be accorded a presumption of validity by a court unless discredited by other evidence. Where a typed or printed form is used, counselors should consider asking the client to make a handwritten statement corroborating that they had carefully considered the typed statement rather than perfunctorily signing it. In every instance, a prudent counselor uses discretion in deciding what is reasonable in the light of the circumstances for his or her practice. The counselor's own testimony about the process, supported by his or her own standard procedure, memory, and notes, and symbolized by whatever document was signed by the client, is likely to be the most important evidence of all.

The final point is that informed consent evolves as the counseling process possibly takes directions other than that described in the initial informed consent. Prudent counselors are alert to these possible changes and get informed consent appropriately.

Establishing, Monitoring, and Terminating Relationships

The quality assurance plan for every counseling practice should include standard procedures for assuring that proper steps are planned and followed in establishing relationships with clients, and for assuring that unplanned and possibly improper steps are not taken. In agencies with more than one counselor, it is important that such standard procedures are understood and followed by every worker. Having such routines also makes documentation easier to complete, and creates less pressure to have extensive written documentation. Additionally, standard procedures provide a context to give specificity for the information provided for informed consent. There is no one set of standard procedures ideal for every setting, and counselors should use discretion in designing and implementing standard procedures for their practice. Because the overall duty of care is based on what is reasonable for particular circumstances, counselors should assure that there is provision for adapting procedures as necessitated by conditions. This chapter provides examples counselors might consider in designing their own procedures.

Establishing Relationships

Counselors should consider when and how the counseling relationship is established. Is everyone who presents with a request for information or assistance considered a client? What screening takes place? How is this process of screening and mutual agreement to form a counselor-client relationship communicated to clients? This process should be clearly articulated and consistently implemented; failure to do so could result in creation of relationships and concomitant duty of care that the counselor never intended. What intake information is sought? Does this information allow counselors to judge the suitability of their services for the client? For example, does it include information about other care the prospective client is getting, any drugs now being taken, and the client's physical and mental condition? It is worth noting that intake information has utility not only for the present obvious purpose but also for future use if a lawsuit alleges that the counselor caused injuries that the counselor's intake procedure identified as existing prior to initiation of a counseling relationship.

In establishing a proper relationship with a client, procedures for getting information about the client are essential. Equally essential are procedures for providing information to the client on the counselor's professional identity, on circumstances of treatment, on client rights and responsibilities, on risks and expectations of treatment, and on alternatives to treatment. It is the provision of such information that assures appropriate informed consent.

Information on professional identity generally should include credentials and experience of the counselor, identity of other professional persons involved in the process, adherence to particular ethical codes, limits of confidentiality, and scope of practice. If supervisors, volunteers, or other persons might be included as part of the process, their professional identity and the limits of their involvement should be described in the beginning, and not left to ad hoc introductions and possibly inadequate informed consent at later times. Information about the nature of the agency sometimes is little attended to in establishing relationships, but it could be a very important part of informed consent.

Information on treatment circumstances might include how a relationship is initiated (for example, that the first session is merely information getting and giving, and that both parties will make a subsequent decision as to whether or not to enter a counseling relationship), any time limitations and or commitments of both counselor and client (for example, that a treatment module consists of 10 planned meetings only, and that the client will be committed to attend at least 4 sessions), accessibility of the counselor, contact from the counselor in case of premature discontinuation by the client, and termination.

Discussion of rights of clients might include asking questions initially and throughout the relationship; preventing the use of certain techniques and being allowed time to consider such; reviewing records; seeking another counselor; and terminating the relationship.

Discussion of responsibilities of clients might include making appropriate commitments of time, money, and energy; understanding and adhering to conditions of counseling; recognizing inherent limitations in counseling; and having reasonable expectations about counseling (that is, do not expect a quick fix).

Discussion of expectations about outcomes should include explicit statements that no outcomes are promised, and that it is possible that clients might not achieve their desired ends from the counseling relationship. Thus disclaimed, certain possible outcomes (for example, increased self-awareness) reasonably anticipated by both parties might be stated.

Discussion of risks of treatment might include the possibility that increased awareness can cause increased pain or discomfort and mood swings. Although this discomfort or vulnerability is likely to be temporary, it possibly could cause disruptions in relationships or other aspects of clients' lives. Counselors should ask clients to pause and give careful consideration before making drastic life changes such as quitting a job or leaving a relationship during the course of the treatment.

Discussion of risks of no treatment might include the possibility that issues not dealt with can continue to cause discomfort to the client. This point is important to raise with clients before counseling is begun, but counselors should use caution in overstating possible risks in light of the voluntariness element of informed consent. Counselors might consider asking clients to consider what the risks of no treatment might be, and to balance these risks with all other information in making their decision.

Discussion of possible alternatives to counseling might include other types of treatment (for example, psychiatry), specialized services (for example, alcohol and drug abuse treatment programs), self-help groups, and no treatment.

Previous chapters have emphasized the fiduciary nature of the counseling relationship, and the impossibility for clients to contract away their rights to receive reasonable professional care and to sue or complain about any perceived failure to receive reasonable professional care. Counselors should never implicitly or explicitly ask clients to indemnify counselors from responsibility based on fiduciary duty. Attempts to do so would be void on their face and also could be deemed to be evidence of misrepresentation or bad faith by the counselor.

However, every counselor-client relationship also has a contractual dimension. Counselors should consider that "good fences make good neighbors" and that it is important to be as clear as possible about business arrangements at the beginning of the relationship. It is not necessary that the contract be written in order for it to be valid. Many of the same statements made about possible advantages or disadvantages of written and oral forms of getting informed consent also apply to contracts. Generally, the contractual dimension lends itself to written documentation to a greater degree than informed consent. Many counselors utilize a contract form stating fee conditions, insurance forms processing methods, and appointment cancellation policies. Counselors should consider information about contract forms (Bullis, 1993), and choose what seems appropriate for their practice. It is recommended that counselors put informed consent information and contractual agreements in separate documents. Again, however, there are no ideal procedures for all to use, and counselors who consider carefully and then decide based on what seems reasonable for their practice are likely to have made the best decision under the circumstances.

Monitoring Relationships

Counselors' quality assurance plans should include being alert to variations in relationships, monitoring business aspects to assure congruence with professional practice standards, and reviewing practice procedures for consistency, safeguards, and documentation.

Counselors should be alert to any variations from the relationship for which the client gave informed consent. Treatment can change according to counselors' professional judgment, new information, clients' perceptions, clients' expectations. New transition points (for example, clients consistently missing appointments, failing to make progress as expected, making better than expected progress) should be noticed and managed. Counselors should take steps to communicate with clients, take appropriate action according to a reasonable standard of care (for example, revise treatment plan, terminate), and get legally sufficient informed consent as changes occur.

On a closely related point, counselors should monitor clients' diligence in taking care of payments or other business matters (for example, returning completed insurance forms). It is possible that counselors' good will might cause them to overlook business details, but there are reasons why quality assurance plans to avoid malpractice should include attention to business matters. Clients' failure to keep up with business responsibilities could be linked with practice considerations in some situations (for example, depression, lack of commitment). Or clients' concern about the bill could cause them to interrupt the treatment routine. In either case, it could be a failure of fiduciary duty of care not to notice and attend to such. It is also possible that clients who accrue large arrearages might be given pause about paying them and continuing in the relationship. Clients' rationalizations could allow them to convince themselves that the counselor has not really earned the payment. Any of these situations have the potential for increasing the likelihood of legal and ethical complaints.

Counselors should review their entire practice procedures from the perspective of legal and ethical quality assurance. Does each procedure exist because it is necessary in order to meet a reasonable standard of care? Have procedures evolved that do not meet legal and ethical standards? Have newly emerged standards been brought to bear on the practice? Is there any practice for which client informed consent has not been given?

Counselors should give particular attention to procedures that might have evolved in response to pressures from the business aspects of the practice. Examples include sending entire records to third-party payers rather than only the specific information necessary to substantiate the claim, or stating diagnoses in terms of third-party payment categories. Counselors should consider the standard of due care and informed consent implications of any business-influenced procedures, and eliminate any procedure that is not consistent with fiduciary duty.

Counselors should review all procedures in terms of their consistency of implementation; clients who notice inconsistency might feel that they have been treated unfairly. In addition, inconsistency makes it difficult to justify particular practices in terms of reasonable care based on professional judgment. One of the most important steps to assure consistency is to make certain that all workers are aware of and adhering to routines that should be followed.

Procedures also should be reviewed in terms of safeguards to assure responsibility for specific actions. Examples include identifying persons who have responsibility for safeguarding records and correspondingly limiting access of other persons to records. Prudent counselors undertake periodic reviews of interoffice communication to assure that all workers are aware of and implementing these safeguards.

Documentation procedures often are a matter of concern for counselors. There is no one rule about how much to document. Counselors should remember that a reasonable standard of care is the controlling rule, and documentation is only part of the care. It is possible that too much documentation could elevate form over substance and actually interfere with meeting the standard of care. It is also possible that too little documentation could be deemed a failure to provide due care to preserve information that might be needed by the client. Counselors should consider possible procedures (Mitchell, 1991), and choose those consistent with the circumstances of the counseling practice and the counselors' professional judgment. As with other procedures, documentation should be done purposefully and consistently.

Terminating Relationships

Counselors should attempt to prepare for termination in such a fashion that there will not be any surprises connected with it, and discussion of termination should be included in the procedures for establishing a relationship. Quality assurance plans should include review of procedures to assure initiating termination at appropriate times, giving clients notice and information regarding termination, facilitating clients' participation in termination, respect for clients' rights to terminate, making any appropriate warnings about risks of premature termination, and making any appropriate referrals.

Termination is a particularly crucial transition point, one often requiring extra human relations attention from the counselor. Processing the termination as a routine part of treatment, routinely attending to any anxiety or disappointments on the clients' part, reviewing progress, planning next steps, and well-wishing all can be important. Getting a certain amount of closure can be important in making the clients feel attended to in a professional manner, and consequently can reduce the likelihood that they might make complaints.

Almost every quality assurance plan should include a routine for requesting final payments. Counselors should require payment when services are rendered, and terminate services to clients who do not pay. However, counselors should be cautioned against suing clients for fees owed the counselor. Persistent attempts to collect a last payment from a client, however justified, seem to invite legal or ethical complaints. Clients who are displeased with the business aspects of the counselor-client relationship tend to express their displeasure in terms of the fiduciary relationship rather than in terms of the contractual relationship. A possible procedure might be to make one request for payment in the same fashion that all other such requests have been made, and then not to make any other requests for payment.

 # Consultation and Supervision

Consultation and supervision, as described earlier, are of major importance in making reasonable standard-of-care decisions and thus in avoiding counselor malpractice. This chapter discusses the importance of getting or giving consultation or supervision in a fashion that allows the consultants or supervisors to provide corroboration or supporting testimony if such should be necessitated. Discussion of consultation and supervision is limited to these purposes alone, and is not intended to state any of the many additional important points about legal issues related to consultation and supervision.

Having a procedure to get consultation or supervision from qualified persons is important. Counselors' quality assurance plans should identify consultants or supervisors who can provide assistance in routine circumstances (although special circumstances might create a need to locate a uniquely qualified consultant). Locating consultants or supervisors should not be done entirely on an emergency or ad hoc basis, with its consequent chance of delay or unsatisfactory results. Some professional associations provide a pool of volunteer mentors in which experienced members agree to make themselves available, within certain limits, to other members needing assistance. Perhaps this custom deserves more attention from local professional counseling associations. Meanwhile, most counselors need to create necessary alliances on their own.

Also important is to make certain that there is agreement on the nature of the assistance to be given and received. Is it supervision (both direct and vicarious responsibility of the supervisor for the counselor's services to the client), consultation (responsibility of the consultant only to the counselor), informal advice giving (no responsibility to anyone, although the advice is seriously given), or mere casual conversation (no responsibility to anyone, and any advice given should not be considered as seriously given)? Do both counselors who are parties have the same understanding of the nature of the interaction? Correspondingly, do both parties have the same understanding of the interaction's legal implications of possibly giving testimony or even sharing in liability for the counselor's conduct? Again, prudence dictates that both parties should clarify and agree on roles at the time of the interaction, and not leave it to after-the-fact clarification if a negligence lawsuit is filed against the counselor.

Both parties should make certain that circumstances allow sufficient contact and communication to enable the services to be effective. Counselors and supervisors who might be liable for any failure to provide due care should agree on the procedure for preserving any necessary evidence about the decision process. Counselors who rely on consultants to be available to give evidence about the decision should either keep notes documenting the consultation or ascertain that the consultant has adequate documentation of the interaction.

It is axiomatic that counselors serving as supervisors have a duty to make certain that they provide supervision only to qualified persons. However, legal prudence dictates that counselors serving as consultants regarding reasonable conduct in counselor-client relationships also should make certain that they provide consultation only to qualified persons. It is possible that an activity deemed consultation by the counselor could afterwards be deemed by a court to have been supervision with its direct-responsibility implications, and any liability problems could be greatly exacerbated if an unqualified person provided the direct services to the client.

 # Training and Supervision of Staff

This chapter discusses training and supervision of staff only as they are related to avoiding counselor malpractice. No attention is given to any of the other important information about legal issues concerning training and supervision of staff.

Counselors could be subject to tort actions based on both direct and vicarious liability for the conduct of their staff members. In terms of direct liability, conventional wisdom and a lengthy legal history merge in the legal principle that persons should be liable for directed acts done by others in the same sense that they are liable for their own conduct. In terms of vicarious liability, conventional wisdom might not be as clear, but the doctrine of *respondeat superior* states a longstanding legal principle that the master can be held responsible for the acts of the servant, even though the conduct was not intended by the master.

Staff members are an extension of professional counselors' services and have corresponding protections. It is necessary for staff members to have access to confidential information about clients, and the legal and ethical protection of confidentiality that applies to the counselor also applies to the staff. For example, it is not possible to subpoena legally privileged information from the counselor's clerical workers any more than it is possible to get it from the counselor.

These legal protections for the staff have corresponding responsibilities for the counselor. Although there are a few public human services settings in which it is a criminal act for any staff person to violate confidentiality of the clients, in most practice settings the counselor bears the responsibility for the conduct of the staff. If the staff is negligent, the cause of action for malpractice lies against the counselor.

Staff members' access to client information, knowledge of and adherence to procedures to protect clients' privacy, and interpersonal skills in relating to clients are the responsibility of the counselor. Every quality assurance plan should include protocol for recruiting, screening, training, and supervising both paid and volunteer staff members. If negligence is alleged, there is no reduction in the standard of care because new staff members or volunteer staff members were involved. Counselors should give extra attention to assure proper conduct of volunteers because they might be deemed to lack the accountability of paid staff. Counselors also should give extra attention to proper conduct of staff members who have access to records or other material that could create a res ipsa loquitur burden for the counselor to prove that any disclosure of the record was not the result of negligence.

Liability Ramifications of Ethical Complaints

Counselors generally are not accustomed to thinking of ethicality in terms of liability, but a prudent counselor is aware that there are possible parallels. In fact, the most problematic aspect of an ethical complaint is that it could be a precursor to legal action. Any complaint, once made, may seem almost to take on a life of its own. As a complainant talks about the process with family and friends, there can be suggestions about seeking legal redress. Sometimes the popular societal myth arises that any wrong, no matter how slight or inconsequential, can form the basis for a lawsuit that will produce a huge money settlement. The result could be that a client who never originally intended to file a legal complaint might decide to do so. Even a client whose ethical complaint is not upheld, and who consequently should logically abandon the complaint as without merit, might attempt to continue to press for vindication through the legal system.

An additional ramification is that a decision about an ethical complaint might have utility in a plaintiff's case if a suit is filed. Although violation of an ethical standard does not equate with legal liability, establishment of an ethical violation might eliminate the defense that a counselor was not only not negligent but had also met the higher ethical standard. Additionally, if the ethical complaint resulted in severe sanctions being applied by a professional organization or a credentialing board, this information could provide a plaintiff's attorney a way to attack both the defendant counselor's credibility as a witness and the wisdom of his or her counseling judgments. Another result from the ethical complaint process that might have utility for a plaintiff is that enlightenment about ethical standards may introduce the idea of application of specialty codes or codes of other professional associations. Most ethical complaint procedures stress confidentiality, and also provide that no ethical complaint investigation will be made if the complaint already is the subject of a legal action. However, courts have extensive power to subpoena records as part of the discovery process once a suit is filed.

Consequently, counselors should have an awareness of ethical complaint procedures, even though their practice indicates good integration of ethical standards at every point. Complaint procedures are not uniform, but generally, a first step is for the client to confront the counselor and seek a resolution. Although a code itself can require this step when a counselor initiates a complaint against a colleague, it can not be required of a client. Further, most clients who lodge a complaint do so after termination, and the counselor has no opportunity to respond until contacted by the professional association or board.

If the complaint goes directly to a state licensing board, the complaint is processed according to the state government's administrative procedure. The procedure usually will not be initiated unless a preliminary check shows that the counselor is licensed by the board. If not, no further action will be taken unless it appears that the counselor has violated some other provision of the licensure law. Usually this process involves sending the report to another arm of government to conduct an investigation. Once the investigation is made and the report is sent back to the board, the board meets to render a decision. According to the particular state's uniform procedure, the board might accept other statements before it renders its decision. The board's decision options are limited by the wording of the enabling statute and implementing regulations as well as by the uniform administrative procedure.

If the complaint goes directly to an association, the procedures of that association and the activity of its leadership in making the procedures viable determine the process and possible results. Most local associations have no procedure for handling complaints and send any received on to the state or national organization. Many state organizations do not have a viable procedure for handling complaints and also send them on to the national organizations. Of course some complaints are made directly to the national organizations. The result is that most of the ethical complaints made about counselors are handled by national professional organizations.

Generally, professional organizations do not initiate allegations of ethical violations on their own and act only when complaints are initiated by some other person. Anonymous complaints are rarely acted on.

A typical procedure for a national organization is to first consider whether the counselor is a member. If he or she is not a member, no further investigation is made. A member, however, is informed of the complaint and given an opportunity to correct any problem that might exist. If the complaint is not settled at that point, typically a detailed, signed statement is requested from the complainant. Then a written notification of the specific complaint is sent to the member and a written response requested. If the member does not respond within a specified time, the association can take action against the member. A member's failure to cooperate in such cases is viewed as a very serious violation itself, and the most severe sanction option is likely. Once the member responds, the complaint and response are given to a select panel of members who individually or as a group are charged with reviewing the material and making a recommendation. The appropriate executive committee of the organization receives the recommendation and pertinent documents, and makes a decision. The options available usually range from finding no violation but rather exemplary behavior, to slight violation with only educative guidance required, to expulsion and permanent barring from membership. The decision then is forwarded to the complainant and the member. There typically is an appeals procedure, with its corresponding review and decision. Because the entire ethical code itself and the procedure enforcing compliance with it are creations of the organization, it is possible that this process could be modified within the organization's change procedures if the professional judgment of its membership indicates that change is necessary.

Remarkably, some state and national professional organizations do not have a procedure for communicating and exchanging information with one another and with state licensure boards. It is possible that certain inequities can occur depending on where a complaint is filed. It also is possible that until there is more consistency and uniformity among the various organizations that receive and process ethical complaints the procedures will be neither well understood nor predictable. Consistent with ethical responsibility to police their profession, and consistent with prudence as practicing counselors, counselors should consider encouraging state and national professional organizations to begin working toward improved communication, consistency, and uniformity. Any such adjustments will primarily be made by the professional groups because state licensure boards have little discretion to make revisions in ethical complaint procedures.

Responding to Legal or Ethical Complaints

There is no one correct way to respond to all complaints. The subject of the complaint, the form of the complaint, and the place where the complaint is filed are all factors to consider in choosing a response. This chapter provides examples of complaints and possible responses. Of course there are many variations on these examples, and counselors should analyze complaints as they are made. For example, clients may not have clearly articulated for themselves what their complaint is, and they often will not have categorized their complaints according to business or treatment matters.

When a client lodges a contractual complaint directly with the counselor, the counselor should respond immediately and forthrightly. Often the matter can be resolved simply, and counselors should consider directly asking the client what solution the client desires. Unless the complaint and its disposition signal a variation in the relationship, no further response usually is necessary.

When a client lodges a fiduciary complaint directly with the counselor, the counselor also should respond directly and forthrightly in a manner that is not defensive or apologetic. Remembering that clients are not customers to be pleased, there might nonetheless be clinical value congruent with due care to ask the client what resolution is wished. In some cases, it may be inconsistent with due care not to ask the client's opinion of possible resolution. The counselor should always be honest concerning treatment decisions, and the counselor should make efforts consistent with due care to resolve the problem in a mutual problem-solving manner. However, unless counselors actually believe that standards of due care were violated, they should use caution and make responses that do not imply violation of any legal or ethical standards.

Counselors should consider including notice about the availability of complaint procedures within the counseling agency and for organizations outside the agency among the points of general information provided to all clients at the time of establishing relationships. However, counselors usually should not volunteer information about other avenues of filing complaints to a specific client who has not asked for it. Doing so could be inconsistent with due care as a suggestion of action that could interrupt the relationship or even as an escalation of a disagreement. If they are asked by the client, counselors should inform the client about appropriate complaint procedures available in the agency or through credentialing boards or professional associations. Every citizen is charged with knowledge of the law. The counselor has no legal duty or ethical responsibility to inform the client about possible legal options available, and the counselor should not present any such information.

If the complaint is resolved satisfactorily with no variation in the relationship, no further action is necessary. If the complaint does signal a variation in the relationship, there is consequent need for the counselor to redefine or terminate the relationship as discussed in previous chapters.

When a client lodges a complaint with an outside organization such as a professional association, there clearly is a variation in the counselor-client relationship. Generally, counselors should not attempt to discuss the complaint with the client; doing so could be deemed as an attempt to unduly influence or coerce the client. An exception is that if the organization itself encourages contact with the client in order to resolve the complaint, the counselor usually should fully cooperate. If the relationship has already terminated, counselors should have no further interaction with the client. If the relationship has not been terminated, counselors should initiate termination, and should have no more interaction with the client than is necessary as part of reasonable care at termination.

Counselors should consider notifying their liability carrier about the ethical complaint. Some policies require it; prudence dictates it at other times. Counselors also should consider whether the circumstances indicate that they should get advice from an attorney at this time. Some professional liability insurance policies, including the one offered by the American Counseling Association, include legal representation when ethics complaints are filed.

When contacted by the outside organization and notified of the complaint, counselors should respond in the fashion and time required by the organization. In every case, counselors should respect the process and attend to its details with scrupulous attention. The response should include all necessary information but no further information. In keeping with the professional identity of the counselor, the tone of the response should be objective and unemotional.

When a client files a lawsuit against a counselor, the counselor should notify his or her liability insurance carrier at once. Failure to do so could result in denial of coverage. Usually, the insuror provides assistance from an attorney, and the counselor should follow that attorney's advice. If a counselor is not provided with an attorney by the insuror, the counselor should seek legal assistance at once, and correspondingly follow that attorney's advice.

With the filing of a lawsuit, the relationship with the client legally has been redefined as an adversarial one between two parties at law. Counselors should not contact the client or take any further actions consistent with the previous counselor-client relationship. Even seemingly innocent contacts with clients or their families could be deemed as attempts to intimidate or coerce. If extreme circumstances regarding the former client's condition indicate that some action should be taken for safety purposes, this information should be communicated to the counselor's attorney. The attorney can advise the counselor about what action to take and can also take action on the counselor's behalf. Counselors should not interact with the client or the client's attorney if they initiate contact. The client's attorney should be referred to the counselor's attorney. Counselors should not discuss the case with anyone other than their attorney or persons whom their attorney recommends (Remley, 1991b). Counselors should be aware that seemingly innocuous comments, such as expressions of sorrow or concern, could be deemed as admissions of fault and, consequently, could be admissible evidence as an exception to the hearsay rule.

 # Liability Insurance

Good practice and good interpersonal skills cannot always prevent lawsuits, and as citizens in this society, counselors have a right to a fair and just trial if they should be accused of a wrong. Note, however, that from a strictly legal perspective citizens have very extensive rights to a fair trial but very limited rights not to have a trial. A popular myth is that if a plaintiff files suit and does not prevail, the defendant then has a strong case to file a suit to recover damages from having been wrongfully sued. Although there are legal causes of action based on abuse of process or malicious prosecution, and although they sometimes are successfully used, it often is hard to get into court with these actions. Further, the burden of proof makes it difficult to prevail if a court should take up the action. The fact is that countersuits generally provide neither a deterrent to the filing of professional negligence suits nor a recourse for defendants who have had to bear the expense of defending such suits.

Our legal system also provides extensive access to the courts for its citizens. Counselors should be reminded that "people can sue other people for anything" (Remley, 1991b), and it is not an overstatement to say that risks of lawsuits or ethical complaints are routine occupational hazards for counselors. The discomfort, pain, guilt, and grief that cause clients to seek counseling can have corollaries of anger, displaced aggression, and projection that increase the likelihood that clients will make legal or

ethical complaints. In addition, it is not surprising to counselors
that some persons have unreasonable expectations of the counseling process, and subjectively blame the counselor for circumstances that anyone objectively should know were not caused by
the counselor. Common examples include the suicidal client's
family who had the family member for 30 years but blames the
counselor who had him for only 30 minutes; the divorced person
who blames the counselor for not saving a marriage that was
already at dissolution stage when counseling was first sought;
and an underemployed worker whose life reflects a pattern of
failing to take advantage of available career development assistance but who blames a counselor for failing to find her a job
congruent with her unrealistic aspirations.

The volatility of issues in today's society also poses additional
danger of lawsuits even in cases where counselors are practicing
with scrupulous attention to legal and ethical standards. Third
parties who have strong feelings about these issues might
encourage a client or a client's family to bring a lawsuit even
when there was originally no feeling on the part of the client or
family that they were wronged.

The threat of malpractice suits has caused some professional
persons to react by deciding not to carry malpractice insurance.
Their rationale is that they might be encouraging the filing of
lawsuits by carrying insurance that could provide a "deep
pocket" of money beyond the resources of the professional
person, and that could thus tempt greedy persons to file suit.
This approach does not seem congruent with prudent counseling practice.

If a lawsuit is filed, defendant counselors must file an answer
in order to prevent the plaintiff client from being given a default
judgment. And even if the defendant counselor prevails, or if the
suit is dismissed as without merit, the expense can be considerable. A simple legal entanglement can result in several thou-
sand dollars of legal expenses. Counselors' quality assurance
plans should include liability insurance to pay for legal assistance if needed. Having such insurance allows counselors to
focus on good practice without undue concern over the possibility of a lawsuit.

Some counselors practice in public settings and believe there
is provision of tort immunity for employees like themselves. In

the absence of a specific statute, however, the doctrine of sovereign immunity disallows suits against the governmental body but allow suits against the employee. The nature of tort immunity, where it exists, is that a statute allows persons having claims against the employee to sue the governmental body instead, disallowing suits against the employee. But tort immunity does not exist in every public setting, and it is likely to have exceptions where it does exist. Counselors should be aware of the specific wording of any tort immunity statute, of the administrative regulations implementing the statute, and of the common practices of the governmental body. In many such settings, counselors might need to carry their own coverage in addition to the limited tort immunity.

There are several factors to consider in purchasing liability insurance (Bullis, 1993), and counselors should consider all of them and make their decision in light of what is best for their circumstances. These factors include sources of coverage, nature of the coverage, and specific exclusions. Sources of coverage include individual policies, additions to homeowners' policies, employee group plans, and professional association group plans (such as ACA sponsored plans). Nature of coverage includes the broad types of claims-made policies that generally cover only those claims made at a time when the policy is still in force, and occurrence policies that generally allow claims to be made at times even after the policy is not in force if the alleged act occurred during the time the policy was in effect. Exclusions can take many forms, but the most common are for alleged intentional acts and alleged sexual misconduct. It is important to note that some policies provide a defense even for excluded acts, even though they will not pay damages if the plaintiff prevails; other policies will not provide a defense for allegations of conduct not included in the policy. Where possible, counselors should purchase policies that provide occurrence coverage and that pay for defending whatever suits might be brought against the insured persons.

If counselors rely on coverage purchased by an employer, they should fully understand the terms of the policy. In some cases the protection is for the agency itself, and the employee receives no individual protection. In agencies such as educational institutions, in which counseling is not the agency's primary purpose, there can be specific exclusions of high-risk activities such as counseling services. The counselors employed in these settings often do not learn about the exclusions unless they persist in seeking information. Additionally, alertness is required about continuation of coverage that does exist because an employer can change or cancel a policy without notifying employees. When there is doubt as to the adequacy of liability insurance coverage purchased by an employer, counselors should purchase their own coverage.

Generally, a counselor who is employed is indemnified by the employer, which means the employer is responsible for actions of the counselor. However, even when the employer is also named, if a counselor is named as a defendant individually in a lawsuit, only if the counselor hires an attorney or has purchased an individual professional liability insurance policy that provides an attorney will the counselor have an attorney who represents him or her alone. In addition, counselors and their employers may have legal interests that are not the same, or are even in conflict. Because conflicts may occur, it is essential that counselors have their own personal attorneys if their name appears in lawsuits.

Counselors should make certain that their liability insurance coverage directly relates to the professional identity used by the counselor in offering counseling services. A policy purchased for a professional counselor could have lowered limits or altered conditions if a later determination is made that the counselor should have been identified as a member of some other profession, such as psychology.

 # Frequently Asked Questions

Q. I'm practicing with scrupulous attention to meeting both the general and specialty ethical standards of professional associations. Isn't this sufficient to avoid malpractice claims?

A. No, not in all cases. Ethical standards state high aspirational standards for the profession, and legal standards state the minimum behavior that society will accept. The two types of standards can coincide, they can exist in parallel fashion with no conflict, they can exist separately with no conflict, and they can conflict. In many cases, meeting the high ethical standards indicates that the minimum legal standards also have been met. However, it is possible to be practicing consistent with the standards of a profession and still be held liable for violating the legal standard of care. It is society's view that controls, not the views of individuals or even professional associations.

Q. Might it not be more effective to ignore ethical standards and only concentrate on legal rules in planning to avoid counseling malpractice?

A. No. The standards of the counseling profession continue to be extremely important evidence of what constitutes legal standards of care, and ethical standards can provide evidence that the profession's standards have been met or surpassed. In determining the overall legal practice standards of a profession, the intertwining relationship of legal rules and ethical standards makes it difficult to apply either one in isolation.

Q. How do I know which of the many possible standards I should follow in making a decision about reasonable action to take in specific circumstances?

A. Counselors should approach decision making about a reasonable standard of care in a systematic way that considers—and balances—the many factors. The formula most often applied to unintentional tort actions is that conduct is wrongful if the burden of alternative conduct that would have prevented the harm is less than the foreseeable probability and gravity of the harm. All of the standards identified provide information about and give meaning to the elements of this formula. However, the decision to be made is not merely which of the standards to follow. The decision to be made is which course of action a reasonable counselor should take in light of all the information applicable to the formula.

Q. In that case, how can counselors always be certain that their conduct will be legally correct?

A. The nature of the counseling profession itself and the nature of our society's legal system make it impossible to always be certain that conduct will be legally correct. As members of a profession, counselors generally must exercise judgment in fulfillment of a discretionary duty of care, and there often is no one clearly correct or clearly incorrect course of action to take. The nature of our legal system is such that courts generally do not give advisory opinions, and sometimes rules are stated by a court in considering what should have been done in a case. If a counselor has prudently made a decision based on professional judgment for the circumstances, in most situations the decision will be legally correct as meeting standards of due care. However, the inherent uncertainty in our legal system is one of several reasons why counselors should maintain professional liability insurance coverage.

Q. Is it possible to limit liability by ignoring possible problems and attending only to circumstances where practice guidelines are clear?

A. Such behavior is likely to fail to meet legal standards of how a reasonable counselor should react to problems. Note that even when counselors react to all the known problems of a situation, it is possible for them to be liable for problems they did not know about. The prevailing rule is that if a reasonable counselor in these circumstances should have known about something, a duty is created just as if there were actual knowledge.

Q. How is it possible to prove something happened or did not happen as part of the counseling process? Isn't it likely to be just one person's word against another's?

A. Popular myth or conventional wisdom might hold that "they can't prove it" in the sense of indisputable acknowledgment of some fact. However, *proof* as a legal term has meaning according to the type of court action, corresponding burden of proof, and legal rules of evidence. In many actual court cases, the evidence consists of the testimony of witnesses, which is often conflicting. When the jury or judge believes the testimony given by a witness, the matter is proved. A counselor's own testimony about the circumstances, supported by his or her testimony about his or her own procedure in attempting prudently to determine reasonable conduct in the circumstances, is likely to have great credibility in a court case. When the testimony is supported by reasonable documentation, the credibility is likely to be even greater.

Q. Can anything be done about the lack of specificity of some standards, the seeming inappropriateness of some standards, and the probability that new standards will continue to evolve whether we like them or not?

A. Professional counselors need not be mere passive recipients of legal standards. Although counselors cannot control or even influence every part of the process, they can and should be active players. The first step every counselor should take is to join appropriate state and national associations, and the second step should be to encourage and support activism in this area. For example, state associations might consider legislative action to clarify case law that sets duties but does not adequately state what behavior will discharge the duties.

 # Guidelines for Practice

If you are approached by someone who asks for your assistance based on your ability as a professional counselor. . .

1. Make certain to give direction to the time and manner of establishing a client-counselor relationship with this person—if your professional judgment is that it seems feasible—in order to clarify roles and provide due care about confidentiality.
2. Do not take any action beyond appropriate referral if your professional judgment is that it does not seem feasible to establish a client-counselor relationship with this person.
3. Do not give help or advice in casual circumstances because it is possible that such behavior could be deemed to create a counselor-client relationship.
4. Do not allow yourself to get held out as acting in your professional capacity when you have not chosen to do so. If someone responds to you in conversation in a way that accords you expert status, disclaim any such status.

When a counseling session reveals information with possible societal importance. . .

1. Respect the confidentiality of the relationship unless the information creates an exception to a reasonable standard of care in maintaining confidentiality. There is no general duty to report past criminal acts, and making such a report could be a violation of a duty of care.
2. Make the appropriate report if there is an exception to confidentiality, such as child abuse.
3. Take appropriate steps to make a report to law enforcement authorities if there is an indication of future criminal activity.

If you are contacted by law enforcement authorities and asked to reveal confidences about a client's past behavior. . .

1. Refuse respectfully to provide any confidential information.
2. Do not, however, take any affirmative action such as providing false information in order to protect clients.

If you practice in a state with a licensing or other statute that establishes privileged communications for counselor-client relationships. . .

1. Know the wording of the statute and its corresponding meaning about the level of confidentiality.
2. Be aware that some statutes make it a crime for the counselor to offer testimony based on a client's confidences in the absence of specific exceptions provided by law.

When you are faced with the necessity of making a decision about reasonable action to take in particular circumstances. . .

1. Remember that counselors generally have a discretionary duty of care rather than a ministerial duty of care, and do not expect clear-cut answers to be found in any standards.

2. Use a systematic approach, take into consideration pertinent standards and other factors, and then make a decision which on balance seems reasonable for the circumstances.
3. Monitor the decision in terms of its effectiveness and possible need for modification or reduction of any injury that occurs.
4. Preserve the information about the process and factors in the process that led to the decision.

When you are holding out to practice as a professional counselor. . .

1. Choose a title with a commonly understood meaning, such as licensed professional counselor, and avoid titles with ambiguous meaning, such as psychotherapist.
2. Do not imply specializations or special skills that you do not intend explicitly to hold out to offer.
3. Remember that the legal standard of care is based on your professional identity, and employers' demands contrary to reasonable practice as a counselor do not excuse counseling malpractice.
4. Obtain professional liability insurance coverage.

When you are designing procedures to assure attention to legal standards of care in establishing, monitoring, and terminating relationships. . .

1. Choose standard procedures to attend to circumstances that may be expected to arise routinely.
2. Make certain that informed consent is prominently attended to in these procedures.
3. Make certain that all professional and other staff persons are aware of and consistently adhering to the procedures.

When a complaint is lodged against you. . .

1. Respond directly, forthrightly, honestly, objectively, and unemotionally.
2. Do not use language that might imply fault when you do not explicitly intend to acknowledge any.

If the complaint procedure indicates a variation in the counselor-client relationship. . .

1. Recognize this change.
2. Behave in a manner consistent with the revised status rather than the previous status.

If a professional organization or licensure board communicates with you about a complaint. . .

1. Respect the process.
2. Attend to its details with scrupulous attention.

If a lawsuit is filed against you. . .

1. Notify your liability insurance carrier at once.
2. Get legal advice and follow it.

Summary

The possibility of lawsuits is a general condition of citizenship in our society, and the possibility of lawsuits based on allegations of malpractice is a routine part of professional practice. However, counselors need not have undue concern or take extreme action in response to this possibility. Prudent counselors' responses can include precautions as part of routine practice.

Every counselor should consider having a quality assurance plan to anticipate circumstances that need attending to, to set procedures for attending to such circumstances, and consequently to reduce the chances for both surprises and mistakes. Generally, the same behaviors that are congruent with counselors' opinions about good professional care for their clients are also congruent with prudent behavior to avoid malpractice. Counselors must remember, however, that their duty as professional counselors is fiduciary rather than merely contractual in nature, and that the duty of care is established and enforced by society rather than by the profession and its clients. Consequently, counselors must systematically consider professional standards of care as part of what they reasonably should know in making decisions for the circumstances.

This broad-based decision-making responsibility, coupled with the ability of our court system to "find the law" and apply it retroactively, makes it impossible ever to avoid malpractice completely. Counselors should consider maintaining professional liability insurance in order to prepare for the unexpected.

 # Discussion Questions

1. What is the overview of a quality assurance plan to practice in a legally correct way? Why is it necessary to study the entire ACA Legal Series or other related texts in identifying pertinent practice issues, standards, and procedures? Why is such a plan necessarily a means to an end rather than an end unto itself? Why cannot counselors merely learn which standards to follow for specific situations? Why did the writer of this monograph take the trouble to disclaim any intended use as legal advice? Why wasn't it sufficient to allow readers to assume that it was educational in nature?

2. What is the nature of legal and ethical standards? How does understanding them in terms of sources, purposes, sanctions, and methods of change help explain the complexity and uncertainty of legal practice standards for the counseling profession? What possible response can counselors make to influence the establishment of legal and ethical standards? Do professional counselors have any responsibility to attempt to give direction to establishment of legal standards?

3. What are the bases of legal liability? What are the elements of an untentional tort? How are these elements established? What meaning does this information have for choosing behavior to avoid malpractice? Why can't a counselor just

get a client to sign a contract that the client won't sue the counselor based on errors in judgment or other disagreements arising from the relationship?

4. Think of a possible counseling situation and analyze it in terms of the elements of an unintentional tort. Is it possible that a court might assign meaning to the elements different from the meaning the counselor intended? For example, if the counselor held out to offer career counseling, was the intention to be held to the standard of care of extraordinary skill as a specialist in addition to all the ordinary skill of a general counselor?

5. If a lawsuit is filed, who determines whether there was or was not malpractice? Whose standards are used? What test is applied to make a decision? Why doesn't a court of law use only those standards established by the profession?

6. Think of a situation that might arise in a counseling session when the counselor's action to deal with one issue might conflict with another issue. For example, what if a client describes unethical or illegal behavior by some past therapist the client had a relationship with, but does not give permission for the present counselor to disclose this information? What systematic approach to making a decision might the counselor use? What factors might be present at each step for the situation you have in mind?

7. Why is it important for counselors to use care in choosing the title they use in holding out to practice? Why should they not use any title as long as it is not illegal to do so? What level of care is expected of a specialist? What should counselors do if they wish to identify a practice narrowly limited in services offered? Why is it important to describe the nature of the employing agency in establishing the counselor's identity?

8. Why should an ethically correct counselor be aware of ethical complaint procedures? What possible implications might an ethical complaint have for avoiding legal complaints?

9. Why are interpersonal skills important in avoiding malpractice? Why are transition points especially important in communicating with clients? How can too much friendliness be possible in dealing with clients?

10. Who can file lawsuits in our society? If someone sues you and does not prevail, what is the likelihood that you can sue and recover the cost of defending the action? Why should counselors carry professional liability insurance? What type of liability coverage is most desirable?

11. Why should counselors offering consultation regarding counselor-client relationships not provide consultation to unqualified persons?

12. How can a counselor be liable for the acts of a clerical staff person whom he or she supervises? What meaning does the term *res ipsa loquitur* have for training and supervision of staff persons?

13. What are the elements of informed consent? If a counselor uses a therapeutic technique that will be of less value if the client knew about it ahead of time, is that sufficient justification not to obtain informed consent? What are the forms of documenting informed consent, and what are their relative advantages and disadvantages?

14. What are some examples of procedures that might be used to establish, monitor, and terminate a professional relationship? Why is informed consent important at each stage rather than merely at the beginning? Why is attention to termination important at each stage rather than merely at the end? Why should counseling practice attention be given to procedures that arise out of the business dimension of the relationship?

15. Is there one set procedure for responding to complaints? Why should available complaint procedures be considered for inclusion in information given at the time of establishing a relationship? Why should information about complaint procedures usually not be given to a complaining client who has not asked for it? What should counselors do first if they receive notice of being sued for malpractice? How should a counselor respond if a former client who is suing for malpractice contacts the counselor and wants to talk? Why is it important not to discuss anything about the case with anyone other than the counselor's lawyer or persons recommended by the lawyer?

Suggested Readings

Bednar, R.L., Bednar, S.C., Lambert, M.J., & Waite, D.R. (1991). *Psychotherapy with high-risk clients: Legal and professional standards*. Pacific Grove, CA: Brooks/Cole. Covers several topics related to legal standards for practice. A unique feature is the inclusion of narratives of sample discussions between a psychotherapist and an attorney concerning possible practice decisions.

Bradley, F.O. (Ed.). (1991). *Credentialing in counseling*. Alexandria, VA: American Association for Counseling and Development. Discusses credentialing from a past and present perspective. Any counselor who forgets—or perhaps never knew—this information might overlook the singular importance for professional counselors of establishing an identity for themselves rather than having someone else establish it for them.

Council for Accreditation of Counseling and Related Educational Programs. (1994). *CACREP accreditation standards and procedures manual*. Alexandria, VA: Author. Every counselor should review the requirements of professional orientation knowledge and attitudes in both the core and environmental standards.

Grundner, T.M. (1986). *Informed consent: A tutorial*. Owings Mills, MD: Rynd Communications. Written for researchers, but valuable for anyone who needs to understand informed consent.

Hogan, D.B. (1979). *The regulation of psychotherapists* (Vols. 1–4). Cambridge, MA: Ballinger. This four-volume set was one of the first extensive treatments of the subject, and it still is one of the most useful in providing a general understanding of the nature of regulating professional practice.

Swenson, L.C. (1993). *Psychology and law for the helping professions*. Pacific Grove, CA: Brooks/Cole. Covers several general topics. Provocative examples and discussions of situations that psychotherapists might encounter are included.

References

Bednar, R.L., Bednar, S.C., Lambert, M.J., & Waite, D.R. (1991). *Psychotherapy with high-risk clients: Legal and professional standards*. Pacific Grove, CA: Brooks/Cole.

Bullis, R.K. (1993). *Law and management of a counseling agency or private practice* (ACA Legal Series, Vol. 3). Alexandria, VA: American Counseling Association.

Cogan, M.L. (1955). The problem of defining a profession. *Annals of the American Academy of Political and Social Science, 297*, 105–111.

Council for Accreditation of Counseling and Related Educational Programs. (1994). *CACREP accreditation standards and procedures manual*. Alexandria, VA: Author.

Hogan, D.B. (1979). *The regulation of psychotherapists: A review of malpractice suits in the United States* (Vol. 3). Cambridge, MA: Ballinger.

Mitchell, R.W. (1991). *Documentation in counseling records*. (AACD Legal Series, Vol. 2). Alexandria, VA: American Association for Counseling and Development.

Remley, T.P. (1991a). An argument for credentialing. In F. O. Bradley (Ed.), *Credentialing in counseling* (pp. 81–84). Alexandria, VA: American Association for Counseling and Development.

Remley, T.P. (1991b). *Preparing for court appearances* (AACD Legal Series, Vol. 1). Alexandria, VA: American Association for Counseling and Development.

Salo, M.M., & Shumate, S.G. (1993). *Counseling minor clients* (ACA Legal Series, Vol. 4). Alexandria, VA: American Counseling Association.

Sweeney, T.J. (1991). Counselor credentialing: Purpose and origin. In F. O. Bradley (Ed.), *Credentialing in counseling* (pp. 1–12). Alexandria, VA: American Association for Counseling and Development.